Visiting Mary

Her U.S. Shrines
and
Their Graces

Julie Dortch Cragon

PUBLISHED BY FRANCISCAN MEDIA
Cincinnati, Ohio

Cover and book design by Mark Sullivan
Cover image courtesy of the author

LIBRARY OF CONGRESS CATALOGING-IN-PUBLICATION DATA
Cragon, Julie, 1960-
Visiting Mary : her U.S. shrines and their graces / Julie Dortch Cragon.
pages cm
ISBN 978-1-61636-654-4 (alk. paper)
1. Mary, Blessed Virgin, Saint—Shrines—United States. I. Title.
BT652.U6C73 2014
232.910973—dc23
2013045146

ISBN 978-1-61636-654-3

Published by Servant Books, an imprint of
Franciscan Media
28 W. Liberty St.
Cincinnati, OH 45202
www.FranciscanMedia.org

Printed in the United States of America.
Printed on acid-free paper.
14 15 16 17 18 5 4 3 2 1

"Entrust to Mary any offering you wish to make to God. In this way, grace will return to its source the same way it came to us.

Certainly, God could give us grace without going through Mary. But he chose not to do so."

—St. Bernard

Contents

Foreword

As a convert to Catholicism, I know firsthand the power and life-changing impact that visiting a Catholic church can have, in particular a church dedicated to Mary. Though it has been more than twenty years ago now, I still vividly remember the first time I ever entered a Catholic church. It was a small, unassuming military chapel in Norfolk, Virginia, called Our Lady of Victory. It may have been tiny and nondescript, but it made a huge impression on me. Indeed, the experience of being in that church was beautiful, personal, and deeply prayerful—and it changed my life forever! That visit ultimately led me to convert to Catholicism, discern a vocation to the priesthood, and begin a lifelong adventure of falling in love with Jesus Christ. To this day, I simply love visiting *any* Catholic holy site dedicated to Our Lady. I am forever grateful for what visiting that little chapel dedicated to Mary did for me.

I have always loved visiting new places. Who doesn't love a good road trip? There's really nothing like heading out on the open road in search of a destination that you have only read about in a book or been told about by a friend. I love the adventure of just spontaneously filling up the gas tank and heading off into the horizon searching for a beautiful place I've heard about but never seen for myself. I think we would all agree that there is something truly fascinating and alluring about discovering new places. We ask ourselves: *What will it be like when I get there? How will I react to it when I see it for the first time? What will it do to me?*

Up until my conversion to Catholicism, though, all of my road trips were secular in nature. They were awesome and memorable, but secular nonetheless. For example, I have memories of attending a concert of a favorite band in a city I'd never been to before, trucking across the USA to see the Grand Canyon, going canoeing in the Ozarks, or heading to a new beach in California to surf perfect waves with friends. Great memories!

But what if there were something more than secular horizons, passing summer excursions, and perfect waves? What if there were road trips that would put us in touch with the persons (Jesus, Mary, the saints) and holy things (sacraments and devotions) that help us get to heaven? Well, my friends, there are, and there are tons of them!

As Julie Dortch Cragon shares with us in this wonderful book, there are countless holy sites dedicated to Our Lady in the US that invite us to visit and experience the adventure of being on a journey to heaven. Don't get me wrong, I love the Grand Canyon, Glacier National Park, weekend excursions to the beach, and all those wonderful experiences that make life so beautiful, but did you know that there are also numerous holy shrines across the US that honor the mother of Jesus and are guaranteed to inspire us to love her, too?

By comparison, in Europe, filled with such cultural richness, history, and natural beauty, people have not only been sightseeing and visiting places like Paris, Tuscany, and the majestic Adriatic coast. For centuries now, they have also been visiting established holy sites dedicated to Our Lady in order to experience a renewal of their faith, a return to the sacraments, and a closer walk with Jesus. This is part of the wonder and universality of Catholicism, and it is offered to us here in the U.S., too!

I have had the honor of being able to personally visit many of the Marian shrines presented in this book: Our Lady of Czestochowa in

Doylestown, Pennsylvania; Our Lady of Good Help in New Franken, Wisconsin; Our Lady of Victory in Lackawanna, New York; and even the Basilica of the National Shrine of the Immaculate Conception in Washington, D.C., where I was ordained a deacon. All these places have been part of my journey and the adventure of growing closer to Jesus, Mary, and my Catholic faith. I simply love that we have so many incredible and holy places we can visit as Catholics!

Even now, as a Catholic priest who speaks and travels all over the world, I love visiting new shrines dedicated to Our Lady. Oftentimes I even extend my stay in a particular area just so I can visit a chapel or grotto that I have only read about. I think it is absolutely fascinating that every single state in the U.S. has holy sites dedicated to Our Lady. Having spoken in all fifty states now, I'm always captivated by the many places dedicated to Our Lady that I discover on the plains, in the cities, near the sea, and in the mountains and valleys of our great nation. Don't you want to discover them, too?

Therefore, as a fellow pilgrim, I encourage you to take up this book and set out on the highways and byways of America to visit Mary in her shrines, grottos, chapels, churches, and basilicas. You will be blessed by these adventures—and you'll remember them for the rest of your life!

—Fr. Donald Calloway, MIC, STL
author, *Under the Mantle: Marian Thoughts
from a 21st Century Priest*

Introduction

Every mother loves to receive a visit from her children. Whether it is planned ahead or because they "were just in the neighborhood," for an extended stay or just for a moment, the time a child takes to stop, to talk, to listen makes a lasting impression, an everlasting memory. Deep in the heart of every child, young and old, is the need for love, a mother's love.

In every state in our beautiful country, there is a place—a grotto, a shrine, a basilica, a church, or a chapel—built in honor of Mary, Our Mother. We all know that we can sit in our homes, cars, offices, or parish church and visit with Our Lady. We ask her to be with us, to intercede for us, to pray for us. But there is something extraordinary about pilgrimage—about making the journey to stop, to talk, to listen.

My family and I have found countless places that have guided us into a deeper relationship with Our Mother. In our travels, we have come to better understand the love that others have expressed toward her and all they have sacrificed to honor her. We have journeyed, and we have found her waiting, so she can bring us to her Son. For several summers, my family and I have traveled through bean fields and cornfields, down back roads and highways, following maps and detours to wonder where in the world Mary is leading us. Countless times we have asked why: Why is this built? Why are we led? Why are others here? And the answer comes time and time again: love. In the words of one of my children, "Mom, you know why. You know. It's all for the love of God."

Through Mary, we are led to that love, to God. Those who experience this type of love want others to share the same experience. And so, I invite you to visit Mary. Here you will find a list of many of the Marian shrines throughout the United States. Included is information about the original appearance by Our Lady along with information from the shrine we visited. The replica shrines here in the United States are beautiful; they are authentic and they offer many graces that Our Lady wants to give her children. Many of us who love Mary and want to visit her shrines throughout the world are not able to travel abroad, so I have prepared a local pilgrimage, complete with the graces and the prayers prompted by the visit. And, even if travel in the United States is impossible, I urge you to enjoy the visit in your own home—fall into our Mother's arms, feel her loving embrace, and be showered with the graces she longs to give you. Take time. Visit your Mother. As we journey through these pages, it is to a place where all are received with open arms, where all are cared for. Where all bring their own needs and desires—or none at all—and she, Our Mother, is there waiting. Some of us have made a plan to stop, and some are just in the neighborhood. Mary understands. And in return for our visit, she gives us her love and her grace and leads us to the greatest gift of love, her Son.

CHAPTER ONE

Our Lady of Grace

Our Lady of Grace is one of the many beautiful titles given to Mary, the Mother of Jesus. As we read in the Gospel of St. Luke, from the moment the angel greeted Mary, "Hail, full of grace, the Lord is with you!" (Luke 1:28), we recognize her as Mother of Grace. For she gives to us the source of grace, her Son, Jesus.

When Mary appeared to Sister Catherine Labouré in the Daughters of Charity convent chapel in Paris, France, Our Lady showed the young sister an image she wanted made into a medal and distributed all over the world, explaining that all who wore it would receive great graces. In the vision, Mary was wearing many rings on her hands, most of which shone rays of light. This image of Our Lady with hands outstretched, standing on a globe and crushing the serpent with her foot, is the image we associate most with Our Lady of Grace. But there are other images with the same title.

In the year 1610, a Carmelite, Dominic of Jesus-Mary, found an oil painting of Mary with the child Jesus and, after having it restored, began praying before the image each night. Wiping some dust from the painting one night, he apologized to Mary for using his rough handkerchief. She bowed her head and smiled. As he fell to his knees, she asked if there was anything he wanted from her. After following her requests of offering up Masses and good works, Mary showed Dominic an image of one of his benefactors being taken to heaven. She told him that all who venerated this picture would receive many graces. Dominic put the image in the Church of Maria Della Scala in Rome, and many people came to venerate Our Lady. The image is now in the monastery Church of Vienna Doabling.

In Cambrai, France, an icon of Our Lady with the child Jesus was brought from Rome under the title Our Lady of Grace. The image is carried through the streets every year on the day before the Feast of the Assumption. Mary's intercession was believed to help put an end to the war between France and Spain in 1529.

In Livorna, Tuscany, the image of Our Lady of Grace was seen by a crippled shepherd boy in 1345. He was asked to carry the picture to the top of a nearby hill, and although he struggled, he did as he was asked. The picture became very heavy as he reached the top, and he sat down to rest. He could feel his crippled leg regain strength, and as he stood, he realized he was cured. He went and showed himself to the village priest, who proceeded to have a shrine built to protect the painting. As the number of pilgrims grew, a larger shrine was built.

Our Lady offers grace to all who come to her. She awaits our visit and our request. Her image is merely a reminder to pray, to ask, and to remember her endless, unconditional love for her children.

. . . .

The Shrine of Christ's Passion
ST. JOHN, INDIANA

Our Lady of Grace stands with her arms wide open, inviting us to visit with her Son, to walk the path of his passion. We have come for our first shrine visit. We are fortunate to meet the man responsible for building the Shrine of Christ's Passion, who tells us the story of his grandfather who first built the shrine to Our Lady—a shrine that stood alone for years at the end of 150 acres of farmland. When the local priest had started looking for property for a new church, suddenly this land, which had been sold forty years prior, became available for purchase. The new church the priest had built on the long stretch of property was named St. John the Evangelist. So, with beautiful symbolism, just as Jesus gave his Mother to St. John from the cross, now St. John watches over Mary from on top of the hill. The field in between was soon changed to a place where all are now welcomed and encouraged to walk the Stations of the Cross—joining Jesus on the path to Calvary.

From the Last Supper to the Resurrection, each step along the way holds a special encounter, as Mary leads us to understand all her Son has done for us. We are given the grace to sit at the table of the Last Supper. We find the apostles asleep in the garden, and we hear Christ ask us for one hour of time in prayer. We listen to the judgment of Pilate, washing his hands of Jesus. The soldier puts the cross on the shoulder of Jesus, and as Jesus falls the first time and again and again, we witness his strength to persevere—for us. Jesus meets his Mother on the journey, and we too meet her face to face. She suffers with her Son, and yet she gives us the grace to continue with him. We are walking, sweating from the heat, contemplating the weight of the cross. There is water along the way that helps us to continue, much like Simon as he helps to carry the cross.

These life-sized figures, these facial expressions, reveal the thirst, the humanity. Veronica wipes the face of Christ, and we in turn are asked to show compassion to those we meet on our journey. Jesus is stripped of his clothing and nailed to the cross. We can do nothing to stop what is happening before our eyes. And then he dies, hanging on that same cross he dragged up this hill, as we hear his last words, "Father, into your hands I commit my spirit." It is done. There is time and a place to sit and to contemplate just what one Man has done for us.

As Jesus is taken down from the cross and laid in his mother's arms, we witness her sorrow. We see him carried to the tomb to be buried. And yet, there is so much more to the story as it continues. Jesus rises and meets Mary Magdalene, just as he meets us daily all along our way, and he asks, "Why are you weeping? Whom are you looking for?" We are looking for him. Even those who do not realize just exactly what is going on in their lives are looking for God. We have journeyed, and by grace we have been led to the one who can best help us find the Lord. Her arms outstretched, Mary welcomes us, and we witness the glorious ascension of her Son into heaven. We notice that the red rose bushes are now white. The sacrifice has been made, and we are blessed by the journey. The farmland has been changed through diligence, faith, and vision—and we too have been changed. It is done. "Father, into your hands…"

Another beautiful title represented at this same shrine is Our Lady of the New Millennium. Carl Demma had a great devotion to Our

Lady. From the time he was a young boy, he carried a holy card of Our Lady of Fatima and prayed the rosary every day. He always wanted to share his love for Our Lady with others because he knew how devotion to her had made an impact on his life. In 1995, Carl commissioned a statue to be made of Our Lady. The thirty-three-foot stainless-steel statue traveled to different parishes throughout the Chicago archdiocese. Carl wanted to inspire Catholics to turn back to Our Lady in prayer for the many needs in this world. He wanted the young to trust her as their Mother and be devoted to her.

Carl participated in the Field of Faith Millennium celebration with Our Lady at Soldier Field in Chicago on June 24, 2000. With nearly thirty thousand Catholics to celebrate Mass with Cardinal Francis George, many bishops and hundreds of priests, this was the largest gathering of Chicago Catholics in two decades. It was an amazing day for Carl to participate with Our Lady. The next day, on the Feast of Corpus Christi, Carl Demma died—and his wife picked up the mission of taking Our Lady out to the parishes.

In 2009, Mrs. Demma visited the Shrine of Christ's Passion for the first time. Moved by her experience, she revisited several times, feeling that Our Lady of the New Millennium should have a place at the shrine. The plaque below the statue reads, "How appropriate that Our Lady of the New Millennium should end her journey here where her Son's journey to Calvary is so powerfully remembered. The Blessed Virgin Mary leads all people to her Son, Our Lord Jesus Christ. You are not here today by accident. Come take the journey."

. . . .

Prayer

Mary, be with us on our journey. Life is filled with good times together at the table with our families and tough times with others who leave us or betray us. Teach us to allow others to help us in our needs. Stand beside us in this world, and walk us through to the glory your Son has prepared. May we give our all in diligence and faith, and as we search, may we always choose Christ, leaving all in his hands.

. . . .

Grace

We are given signs and opportunities every day. If we walk with eyes wide open and venture out of our comfort zones, great things can happen. One short journey, one stop along the way, one encounter, one great thing, can change our lives.

. . . .

CHAPTER TWO

Ave Maria

. . . .

We begin our prayer to the Virgin Mary with Ave Maria (Latin), or Hail Mary, asking her to pray for us in this life and at the hour of our death. Again, Hail comes from the greeting of the angel Gabriel to Mary at the Annunciation. "Hail, full of grace, the Lord is with you!" (Luke 1:28). He then calms her, "Do not be afraid, Mary, for you have found favor with God" (Luke 1:30). This amazing greeting from the messenger sent by God announces the coming of our Savior: "And behold, you will conceive in your womb and bear a son, and you shall name him Jesus" (Luke 1:31).

The second part of the greeting comes from Mary's visit to Elizabeth: "Blessed are you among women, and blessed is the fruit of your womb!"

(Luke 1:42). From this first greeting, what becomes for us a prayer, we rejoice with Mary and we call upon her because she is chosen by God to bring us his Son, the Savior of the world. Mary shares with us the importance of a visit, of spending time, and she always shows us the way to her Son.

. . . .

Ave Maria Grotto
CULLMAN, ALABAMA

Many times we have read the sign on Interstate 65 South directing us to visit the Ave Maria Grotto, and many times we have passed by, too busy on our way to another place. This day is different. This day my daughters and I take the time to make our first visit to this grotto built in honor of Our Lady. It was clearly built for us to enjoy, to explore, to take time with one another.

The Ave Maria Grotto consists of a huge main grotto, or cave, surrounded by 125 miniature structures of biblical scenes, famous buildings from around the world, and Marian apparition sites. Often referred to as "Little Jerusalem," the four-acre park is the work of Brother Joseph Zoettl, a Benedictine monk who built the first replicas in 1912 as a hobby to pass time while working in the monastery powerhouse shoveling coal into the furnaces. His small creations were placed out in the gardens, capturing the attention of some of his fellow brothers and their guests. As their popularity grew, the scenes were moved to the former rock quarry, and Br. Joseph was asked to build grottos to sell in the store at the college. He made more than five thousand small grottos before starting the large central Ave Maria Grotto in 1932. People sent him materials from all over the world, including marbles, glass, old jewelry, tile, beads, even cold cream jars and toilet tank floats. Br. Joseph's creative use of donated materials can be found throughout the grotto.

The girls and I venture forth with our self-guided tour pamphlet into the world Br. Joseph created for us. Reading every sign and searching for all the materials donated to make each of the miniatures, we settle into a fascinating journey of one man's love for Mary and Jesus and the world God created. The girls are constantly pointing out small details and trying to see inside the buildings, noticing stained-glass pieces, Della Robbia plaques, and statues of saints and angels. We walk and talk about the Old and New Testament scenes, the abbeys and monasteries and churches. We walk through Rome and the Holy Land and visit the shrines of Our Lady of Lourdes, Fatima, and Guadalupe.

As we read about Br. Joseph's life, his call to be a monk, his fears and feelings of loneliness as he left his home in Bavaria for a new life in America, we understand a little more about his complete dedication to the work of this grotto. He lived as a small, quiet, humble man waiting to find his calling, searching for a place to use the gifts God had given him.

We kneel at the huge Ave Maria Grotto, the central grotto, even though the name encompasses the entire park. The Blessed Mother holding the child Jesus is the main figure inside the grotto, with St. Benedict and St. Scholastica, twins who founded the Benedictine orders of monks and nuns, kneeling on either side. The opening contains a large marble altar covered in a mosaic of crushed glass, stones, and shells. Miraculous in construction, this place made to honor Our Lady was no small task at twenty-seven feet in height, width, and depth. There were no plans for Br. Joseph to follow as he built this monument in honor of Mary and Jesus. He merely followed his heart to put together a place where thousands of people come each year to see the wonder and beauty of God's creation poured out through the use of his hands and the talents God gave to him. His work truly reveals an act of love.

After sharing details of our visit with my mother, she reminds me of the small rock grotto on one of her balconies. I can picture it on the patios of each of our previous homes. She tells us that my grandfather did some plumbing work for the Brothers in Cullman well before I was born, and as payment, he received one of Br. Joseph's mini grottos. Suddenly our time at the grotto means more than just time spent off the Interstate. We have a personal connection, a reminder of the past and of time spent and talents shared.

. . . .

Prayer

Mary, Our Mother, may we learn to take the time to listen to God's call. Today we kneel and dedicate ourselves to finding time in our busy lives to stop, to pray, to serve. Help us, Blessed Mother, to listen for the greeting, the announcement, and to answer with a simple yes. As we begin each journey in our lives, may we feel calmed in your presence, knowing that we are safe in your loving arms. In some small way, help us to make a difference and like you, to lead others to your Son.

. . . .

Grace

We are all in search of our calling. We are all at some point trying to reach our potential. Often, out of fear, we hold back, wondering what others may say or think. We pass by opportunities thinking we are just too busy, too overwhelmed. It could be a simple yes, and yet we miss the message, the sign. Today, we have stopped, and today we have listened and learned. The work of our hands is our calling, our potential, our connection.

CHAPTER THREE

. . . .

Our Lady of Lourdes

. . . .

Our Lady appeared to Bernadette Soubirous, a fourteen-year-old peasant girl, on February 11, 1858, in Lourdes, France. Bernadette was gathering firewood with her sister and a friend when she became weak because of her asthma. Falling behind the other girls and walking alone, she suddenly heard a rushing sound and noticed a woman standing in the cave at Massabielle. Bernadette described her as a beautiful lady dressed in white, with roses at her feet and holding a rosary. The young girl knelt before the Lady, and together they prayed.

Our Lady appeared to Bernadette eighteen times, telling her to "pray for sinners" and stressing the importance of penance. She told Bernadette to dig in the ground and to drink from the water that came up through the dirt. Although it was quite muddy, Bernadette did as Our Lady requested, and the next day a spring was flowing from the spot. The following month, a woman was cured by dipping her crippled hand into the spring. Many have been cured from the water that continuously flows in Lourdes to this day.

Although Bernadette was questioned and tormented by skeptics, her story never changed. She instructed the priest to build a chapel at the site near where Mary appeared, and the priest told Bernadette to ask the Lady her name. When she asked, Mary responded, "I am the Immaculate Conception." Knowing that Bernadette would never have known that title from anywhere else, the priest believed that this was truly Our Lady.

Today, millions of pilgrims still visit the grotto and the basilica, where processions are held at night and the rosary is prayed in many languages. Many grottos are built as replicas of the Grotto of Our Lady of Lourdes at Massabielle. All are built out of love for Mary, and all seem to bring peace and some type of healing. All are reminders of Mary's appearances to Bernadette and the messages she gave to the young girl to spread all over the world. Fast. Pray the rosary. Go to confession.

. . . .

National Shrine Grotto of Our Lady of Lourdes
EMMITSBURG, MARYLAND

In the mountains of Emmitsburg, Maryland, about five hundred yards from Mount St. Mary's College and Seminary, Mary waits at the grotto for those seeking peace, seeking a place for quiet prayer and reflection, seeking comfort. Drawn by a "light in the mountain," Father John Dubois, a priest from France, founded the natural grotto, formed from the water flowing off the mountain through the base of a huge oak tree. In the early 1800s, he erected a cross there.

Standing on the hill overlooking the valley, my daughters and I sense that we stand in a special place, a quiet place, a peaceful place, despite the coming and going of groups of people. Entering the pathway to the grotto, a huge golden statue of Our Lady of Grace marks the place where Fr. Dubois built the original church on the hill in 1805. We stand before her, and each of us remarks about Mary's face, which seems to display a look of anger. We touch on her sadness for our world today.

But as we move closer and look straight up from below the statue, we can see that she smiles down upon us, almost as if to say she is glad we have come to visit her at this grotto. The stone path is lined with the Stations of the Cross, set back in nature with a simple wood cross on the stone, a reminder of the crosses attached to trees as the paths were cleared up the mountainside. As we walk, we notice an elderly man being helped all along the path to get to Our Lady's Grotto.

The replica of the Lourdes Shrine in France was built on the mountain in 1875 under the direction of the president of St. Mary's College. Entering the sanctuary of the grotto, we see signs that request silence, a silence we can only imagine St. Bernadette experienced with Mary as she prayed in her presence and as she listened with her heart. At the grotto, Our Lady stands with hands folded in prayer with us and for us to the Father. Her sweet face seems to call us forward. Her invitation to us is the same as it was to Bernadette: "Do penance and pray for sinners." The young and old, the sick and those who care for them, all gather at the altar and write prayer requests to Our Lady for her intercession. They light candles to honor her. A young woman sits praying the rosary, just as Our Lady requested for the reparation of sin. All ages and many different nationalities are spread throughout the pathways.

St. Elizabeth Ann Seton came to the mountain in 1809 and often taught and ate meals at the grotto. Today, as children wander around the stone walls, we can envision Mother Seton and her sisters who would "ramble for a time around the grotto" and "amuse themselves until time for Vespers and Benediction."[1]

The path past the grotto ends with "the Calvary Group," a shrine built to honor Fr. Dubois for his courage. Gazing upon her Son and his crucifixion, we know that Mary is always leading us to him, showing us the way to him. She has shined the light deep in the mountains and has helped to carve the path to ease our journey, through the work of others, through the faith of those who have gone before us.

Following the path back down past the grotto, there is a tiny stone chapel built where once stood the large oak tree whose roots formed the original grotto. Those who visit kneel before the tabernacle where the words are written, "You are now alone with him in this chapel. Speak to him now while you may." The well-used kneelers tell of the history, the love, the time spent with him in this place where once Fr. Dubois spent time in the original grotto. We witness a young man in the chapel who has left his shoes at the door and who kneels at the tabernacle for some time. As he leaves, he bends and kisses the words that suggest we take the time to speak to Jesus, to pray and to beg pardon while we are right in front of him.

The stairs outside the chapel lead down to the pool of water surrounding another statue of Our Lady. In 1861, Father Obermeyer and two seminarians built a dam above the Lourdes Grotto and ran a water line to this basin below the chapel. Pilgrims fill their jugs and jars with the springwater that pours from the spigots in the stone wall. They fill their hands and wash their faces. They kneel before the giant pool of spring water and ask Our Lady to intercede, to bless, and to care for their needs. Again, despite the number of people, there is silence at this place.

The final walkway includes the mysteries of the rosary in beautiful mosaics as well as several small shrines to Our Lady under various titles. The quote from St. Louis Marie de Montfort appropriately leads us to prayer: "For myself, I know of no better way of establishing the kingdom, Eternal Wisdom, than to unite vocal and mental prayer by saying the Holy Rosary and meditating on its Fifteen Mysteries."[2]

We witness many who stay for long periods on their knees at the grotto and at the small shrines along the pathways. As we continue on our way, a family remains at the grotto, teaching their children to pray just as Mother Seton once taught her sons and the children from the valley. We witness water being poured into jugs at the huge pool built to gather the water from the mountain spring. We witness the obvious flow of graces for those who help the sick and the aged and all who cannot help themselves.

· ·

Our Lady of Lourdes Shrine
EUCLID, OHIO

We are delivering a statue in Ohio when the man we meet suggests we visit Our Lady of Lourdes Shrine, which is not far from his business. The shrine was opened in the 1920s by the Good Shepherd Sisters. A replica of the Lourdes Shrine in France, it is a convenience for those who would like to visit where Our Lady appeared but cannot journey to another country. The shrine is now run by the Sisters of the Most Holy Trinity and is a beautiful place for rest, peace, and prayer. We take this opportunity to walk to the base of the hill where the shrine welcomes us to take time.

The air is damp and cold as we walk the hill to the Stations of the Cross and the rosary walk. The busy season is well past, and yet there are visitors like us who just happen to be in the neighborhood. Seems we are often in need of a little suggestion, a gentle push to stop in our day and take time for God. We had no intention to make this short visit, and, as usual, we are grateful. Our Lady, Bernadette, the altar, the crutches and braces and rosaries left in thanksgiving, and the beautiful chapel bring peace, and we are reminded that we can stop any time, any part of the day, and make a short visit and invite others to do the same.

. . . .

Oblate Mission's Lourdes Grotto and Our Lady of Guadalupe Tepeyac de San Antonio
SAN ANTONIO, TEXAS

My daughter and I are talking in our hotel room about things to do in San Antonio, when a paper falls out of my journal with information about the Oblate Missions and the shrines on their property. She simply says, "Let's go." We have come this far in our journey, and we might as well follow all the signs that lead us to what we believe Mary wants us to accomplish. We arrive at the Oblate Renewal Center and go directly to visit the shrine. We walk the stairs to visit Our Lady of Guadalupe, where we find a place that many have visited, lit candles, left rosaries, and written requests. The shrine is beautiful, set up at the side of the Lourdes Grotto, which we visit next.

The area has become the spiritual center for the Oblate Missions, a place to pray for people in need and for those who care for them all over the world. There have obviously been many before us and many to come, from the number of chairs and cars. As we have found many times, there is someone kneeling in prayer at the shrine, alone, quiet, in need. This person turns to ask me for something, and I don't really pay attention. I am wrapped up in my own visit. We go to the interior of the Lourdes grotto and find a door that leads to a small chapel, an Adoration chapel. We are richly blessed with God's presence.

Completely disconnected with the idea of the missions and the work they do all over the world, while visiting in the presence of Christ I cannot get my mind off the man who was at the grotto. We return before we leave, and he is still there. We take one last moment before Our Lady and have one last encounter with the visitor, one of the possible reasons that the paper fell, one of the possible gifts of opportunity. Again, we are blessed in God's presence.

"Ask Mary for the grace to love Our Lord as she loves him and to remain faithful to him in life and in death."

—St. Bernadette

. . . .

Prayer

Mary, our Mother, we come to you in need of healing, in need of repair from all that the world seems to load upon us. Help us to constantly be in search of that "light in the mountain," that opportunity. Help us to constantly be open to that call to bring others to you. You seem to clear the path that leads us back to your Son. Help us to stay close to that path, to not lose our way and to work on your requests that we pray the rosary, fast, and confess our sins. Help us to take care of one another.

. . . .

Grace

At the shrine, one witnesses people's beliefs in the miracles. A barefoot man leaves his kiss, a symbol of his love for Our Lady, at the altar; a family tucks their personal needs, their personal messages in the grotto; and a man in need simply knows someone cares. In a world filled with noise and confusion, in a world filled with stress, in our busy lives, despite people everywhere, despite overflowing calendars, Mary gives us the grace to find rest, to find peace, to find answers. She gives us the opportunities to stop and to take time. She gives us her Son. Sitting in our homes, kneeling at the tabernacle, visiting her at the grotto, praying the rosary, we witness.

CHAPTER FOUR

. . . .

Our Lady of the Miraculous Medal

C ome to the chapel. The Blessed Mother awaits you." On July 18, 1830, Sister Catherine Labouré, a novice at the motherhouse of the Daughters of Charity of St. Vincent de Paul, in the Rue due Bac in Paris, was led by a small child through the hallways to the convent chapel. As they approached the altar, she heard a rustling sound, and Our Lady descended and sat in the chair near the altar. Catherine knelt beside her and, putting her hands in Mary's lap, listened for several hours. Mary explained that God had chosen Catherine for a mission. It was a mission that would be contradicted, but one that God would give her the grace to fulfill. She would only be allowed to tell her spiritual director and no one else. She also told Catherine of the evil in France and in the world.

During evening meditations on November 27, Sr. Catherine again heard a rustling sound, and the Blessed Virgin Mary appeared inside an oval frame, standing upon a globe, holding a gold ball, and wearing many rings with rays of light coming down from them. Around the frame were the words, "O Mary, conceived without sin, pray for us who have recourse to thee." As the frame rotated to the back, Catherine could see a circle of twelve stars, a large *M* surmounted by a cross, and below it two hearts, one crowned and one pierced with a sword. Catherine asked Our Lady why some of her rings did not shed light, and she explained that those were the graces for which people forgot to ask. Catherine was asked to describe the image to her confessor, Father Aladel, and to instruct him to make medals to be distributed all over the world, with the promise that all who wore them would receive great graces.

Catherine took the information to Fr. Aladel and asked him to have the medals made, as Our Blessed Mother requested. After two years of investigation, the medals were made and distributed, though the apparitions were not revealed until forty-six years later, when Catherine was nearing death. After many conversions, cures, and answered prayers, the name of the medal changed from Mary's Immaculate Conception to the Miraculous Medal.

. . . .

National Shrine of Our Lady of the Miraculous Medal
PERRYVILLE, MISSOURI

God has a plan for us that we may not understand at the moment. As the day unfolds, however, we often come to see clearly his amazing grace. He tends to lead us on paths we may never have journeyed on our own.

As my husband, three of our children, and I drive into the parking lot of St. Mary of the Barrens Church to visit the National Shrine of Our Lady of the Miraculous Medal, we wonder whether we are in the right place. We have traveled through the cornfields and what we suspect to be the soy fields of Kentucky to Missouri to arrive in a place with only one other car in the parking lot. The summer heat keeps us from hopping out of the air-conditioned car until we are sure there is something to see. Noticing the visitor center, we decide to seek clarification, and the nice lady behind the counter of the gift shop confirms that the shrine is inside St. Mary of the Barrens Church across the parking lot. Telling us that we can take a self-guided tour, she directs us to a wall filled with pamphlets about the history and the different areas on the property.

The church is simple from the exterior, but as we pull open the front doors in search of cool air, we open ourselves to the beauty and history of the Vincentian order and the Miraculous Medal. The church is lined on each side with altars or chapels dedicated to the saints and special devotions of the Vincentians and the Daughters of Charity. My husband and I start meticulously moving from chapel to chapel, enjoying the beautiful paintings that fill the walls and ceilings and tell stories of the saints and their missions. Our younger two children rush from one area to the next, reporting back with interesting tidbits of information, such as descriptions of the old holy water receptacles and sacrariums in the sacristy. Several times they report that their sister is just sitting in the Miraculous Medal Shrine. As I catch a glimpse of her across the church, I cannot help but think how wonderful it is that she is so comfortable, so settled in with Our Lady.

But we continue, learning about the great saints and their missions. The second chapel, the St. Vincent de Paul Chapel, speaks of his care of prisoners and his service to the poor and to orphaned children. It was this priest's face in a dream that initially drew St. Catherine to join the Daughters of Charity. The paintings portray his love and his charity. The Passion Chapel further explains Vincent's call to see Christ in those who suffer.

The Miraculous Medal Shrine is the third chapel on the right of the church. Rounding the sanctuary with a beautiful reproduction of Murillo's *Assumption of the Virgin* and pausing at the St. Joseph Chapel, we find our daughter still sitting with Our Lady. I drink in all the information about the shrine's being added by promoters of the association in 1929–1930 in order to replace an older shrine to Our Lady. Like thousands of previous pilgrims, I am welcomed by the words, "Come to the foot of this altar. Here graces will be showered on all."

I am fascinated by the way the front and the back of the Miraculous Medal form the shrine. Our Lady stands above the altar, with rays coming from her hands, ready to send the graces that await those who ask. In the archway, we read the words, "O Mary, conceived without sin, pray for us who have recourse to Thee." In the base of the altar I spot the large *M* surmounted by a cross (Mary intercedes for us to God) with the twelve stars. On the tabernacle doors are the two hearts, Jesus's crowned and Mary's pierced by a sword, to complete the back of the Miraculous Medal.

Our Lady's appearance to St. Bernadette is also painted within the shrine. Bernadette was wearing the Miraculous Medal when Our Lady appeared to her in Lourdes, France, and revealed herself as the Immaculate Conception, the same words she spoke to St. Catherine years earlier. Throughout the chapel are images of St. Catherine giving out medals to the people of Paris, kneeling in conversation with Our Lady, and being asked to have the medals made. Over and over, I think about Catherine keeping these visions a secret for forty-six years, not telling anyone but her confessor. My daughter asks if she can light a candle, and I promptly drop some money in the box. Above the offering is a beautiful prayer for lighting a votive candle, which asks that the light be used in service to Our Lady for whatever purpose may be revealed. The prayer focuses on making us loyal and faithful in our lives and asks that we may be consumed in the light and warmth of Mary's love.

The younger children are getting restless to go outside, so my husband accompanies them, as I finish visiting the last few chapels of St. Louise de Marillac and the Little Flower. I venture back to let my daughter know we are going outside and find that there she remains with Our Lady, content. I cannot help but picture Catherine, kneeling with her hands in Mary's lap for hours, listening to her, content. How wonderful to see this young girl also resting at the base of Our Lady's open arms. "Mary, give her the grace to do God's will."

Soon, we are all together outside, and we walk to the small log cabin built by Father Joseph Rosati and his small group of Vincentian missionaries who ventured from Bardstown, Kentucky, in 1818 to build a seminary at the request of the people. Strange to think that they were building a place that would eventually be dedicated to spreading devotion to the Miraculous Medal years before Our Lady appeared to Catherine Labouré. The new church was built in 1837, but the Shrine of Our Lady of the Miraculous Medal was added almost one hundred years later.

As we follow the path, we pass a small sign that directs us to the large outdoor grotto of Our Lady of the Miraculous Medal. On the post hangs a simple chain with a large multicolored heart on the end, symbolizing to me someone giving her whole heart in love for Our

Lady. As we approach the grotto, we can see bouquets and vases of flowers left in honor of Mary. A huge white statue of Our Lady is above the altar, and images of the front and back of the Miraculous Medal are embedded in the limestone below the statue and on either side of the altar. The grotto, once the rock quarry used to build St. Mary of the Barrens Church, is another quiet place to rest at the base of Our Lady's open arms.

Zoe Labouré—later St. Catherine—was the ninth of eleven children, and, when she was nine years old, her mother died. After the funeral, Zoe pulled a statue of Mary off the shelf in her mother's room and, speaking to her, said, "Now, you will be my mother." Years later, when she was twenty-four years old, she rested her hands in Mary's lap and listened intently to all that she was instructed to do. Yes, St. Catherine Labouré leaves us with the Miraculous Medal, but she also leaves us with her example. She has inspired us to put our trust in our heavenly Mother, sit with her, obey her, and ask her for the graces to endure, to overcome, to believe, and to love. Mary intercedes for us to her Son. Ask for the grace. The Blessed Mother awaits you.

. . . .

National Shrine of St. Elizabeth Ann Seton
EMMITSBURG, MARYLAND

Elizabeth Ann Seton converted to Catholicism after the death of her husband. With her children, she moved to Maryland to open a school for girls at the request of the seminary in Emmitsburg. She started the Sisters of Charity—following the rules of the Daughters of Charity of St. Vincent de Paul—and she established the Catholic school system and worked with the poor. She and her sisters frequently visited the Grotto of Lourdes founded by Fr. Dubois.

We too have come to visit the grotto and have happened into the Shrine of St. Elizabeth Ann Seton. Opening the doors to the basilica, we are pleasantly surprised to find covering the wall behind the altar the huge mosaic of Our Lady giving the Miraculous Medal to St. Catherine Labouré. The shrine is a tribute to the work of charity, and we are quickly reminded of the work that Our Lady calls us to do in this world: to educate, show compassion, serve, and visit. We find in Elizabeth Ann Seton an example of answering that call. This incredible shrine, which recalls the work of the sisters during some of the most difficult times in our history, stands as an example to us of how one woman can make a difference by following the call of Christ.

. . . .

Prayer

Mary, we ask you to give us the wisdom to know the will of your Son for our lives and the grace to do what he asks. May we feel comfort sitting with you so that we may come often and allow you into our lives. With your help, with the grace you have to give us, we can persevere in a life that some days seems impossible. Give us the gift of peace. Teach us wisdom and love, and give us the courage to pass it on to one another.

. . . .

Grace

Mary comes to us in simplicity, and as we open ourselves to receive the grace she offers, we open ourselves to her beauty and her deep love. Beyond the doors of the plain, past the fields of the ordinary, there are amazing gifts of peace and of tranquility and of grace. Mary invites us all to rest our hands in her lap and allow her to take care of us.

. . . .

CHAPTER FIVE

Share the Healing and the Hope

Our Lady of the Snows

· ·

In August 352, a Roman patrician and his wife, having no heirs, prayed that Our Lady would make known to them what to do with their wealth. That night in a dream, Our Lady asked for a church to be built.

The next morning, the couple awoke to find that, although it was summer, snow had fallen on Italy's Equiline Hill. Pope Liberius had had the same request in a dream, and he agreed that the snowfall was a sign from Our Lady. Basilica Liberius was built and dedicated to Our Lady of the Snows. The basilica was later restored by Pope Sixtus III and renamed the Basilica of St. Mary Major of Rome. To celebrate the dedication, white rose petals were dropped from the dome during the Mass. Inside is the icon of Mary, Salvation of the Roman People, believed to have been painted by St. Luke.

. . . .

National Shrine of Our Lady of the Snows
BELLEVILLE, ILLINOIS

Quiet places of prayer renew our strength for the journey. God knows our needs.

The more-than-100° temperature does not deter our family from wandering the acres of land settled for the pure purpose of honoring Mary. We are not the only pilgrims who have braved the heat, for, as we enter the Church of Our Lady of the Snows, a rather large group of people are talking with one another, just after Mass. The contemporary space is welcoming and wide open, but we find quiet in two small spaces along the walls. Drawn first to the tabernacle, we kneel and spend a few moments just being thankful for the journey. As the piano is practiced in preparation for another Mass, I feel distracted, but my children seem to pray right through it, undisturbed.

As we leave, I notice the beautiful statue of Our Lady, and as I look into her face, I find peace in her eyes. She wants us to stay for a while and to experience devotion to her as it was first brought to the area by Father Paul Schulte when he came to St. Henry Seminary in Belleville in the 1940s. It is funny to me that St. Henry is also the name of our parish church at home. Fr. Paul, a pilot who brought medical supplies to remote Oblate missions in the Arctic Circle, had a great devotion to Our Lady of the Snows. He commissioned a picture of her surrounded by the rays of the northern lights, including the airplane he used on sick call visits to an Inuit mission. The painting was placed in the chapel of the seminary, and as devotion to Our Lady of the Snows grew, the Oblates decided to build this shrine in her honor.

I stand before the face of Our Lady as she presents her Son, and I feel the invitation from her to block out the sounds, to pull away from the crowds, if only in my mind and my heart, and to stay and allow the feeling of comfort she offers. As we walk outside the church, my daughters are at the ready to light candles for the intentions of one of our family members. I welcome the act, feeling it gives them a sense of doing something for someone else. I love to light candles and watch the smoke lift my prayers and my requests up to the One who loves me unconditionally, despite my shortcomings, my lack of trust, my touch-and-see-to-believe faith.

We can see the main shrine with the huge *M* on top of the shell surrounding the descending dove. We move toward this beacon as if it is guiding us, leading us in. As we get closer, we see once again Our Lady presenting her Son to us, as if to assure us that he is here, right here just for us as we visit. She is surrounded by a gold chalice, and we read that the rings and circles in the stonework all around her symbolize the blessings from Christ to all who receive him. "Come to the table. Take and receive." The wide-open invitation is for us all.

As we move down behind the shrine, we find the Christ the King Chapel. Five large mosaics cover the walls, with the tabernacle front and center before them. We've come to him once again because of his mother. She has led us to this small, quiet haven from the grand outdoors. The silence allows our hearts to speak to his. This is where peace can be found. I feel we have come to the heart of the shrine. There are images of other apparitions of Mary along the back wall. These images hold rosaries and medals and notes from visitors, asking Our Lady to intercede for them to her Son, from their heart to his.

The next chapel is for her. She stands in the silence amid large, flowing, brightly colored angels. She requests a shrine to be built in our hearts, a place we can go anytime during the rush of the outside world and sit in peace and speak to her Son. Once again, she presents him to us as a gift to ease us from our sorrows, our pains, our worries in this world. We are among the celestial, surrounded by the protection of Our Mother. Down here, in the heart, we would never know the outside world exists.

Outside the chapels are rosary courts, with mosaics depicting the joyful and glorious mysteries of the rosary. The kneelers in each area give pilgrims the space to pray, to linger. The candles are lit, and the prayers are lifted.

The Millennium Spire, which rises out of the Candelarium (a building filled with candles pilgrims have lit in prayer), was built in response to Pope John Paul II's preparation for Jubilee 2000. Names of donors cover the platform, and somehow my husband has spotted the names of two long-ago friends, a salesman and his wife, directly in the center of the shrine. The names make us pause in prayer at the base of what seems a massive candlewick that reaches to the heavens.

The hill goes over to the Mother's Walk Garden around the Annunciation Garden, surrounded by roses with a pond holding four huge bells. Our favorite walk down the hill through the woods leads to the grotto of Our Lady of Lourdes. We find the cave—two-thirds the actual size of the grotto in France and sprayed to look like stone—a welcome relief from the heat.

We dare not leave the shrine before visiting Our Lady of Guadalupe Hill. The first thing we notice are the rosaries hanging from Our Lady's hands, obviously left by grateful pilgrims. Again, the backdrop is built in such a way that we feel alone with her among the rocks and the cactus. Walkways lead to the Stations of the Cross, with a separate devotion area to the Agony in the Garden, finally ending with the Empty Tomb and the Resurrection.

In the blazing summer heat, we realize that the place that marks where we should build a shrine is not on a hill far away, but in our hearts. The answer comes once again from Our Lady of the Snows's wide-open invitation to build a shrine—at the center of which is the heart of her Son.

. . . .

Prayer

Mary, Our Mother, at your request a shrine is built, and by faith people visit in search of your Son's will for their lives. And as if in a dream, when we are quiet, we find answers. At the heart, we all have times we need to feel refreshed and renewed and reconciled. Even when we don't know it, we can use that extra gift of grace that comes when we find the heart of Christ.

. . . .

Grace

Somehow, children find a way of finding peace amid the noise of this world. They can block out all the things that tend to irritate the adults and find in their hearts the place meant for hearing, for listening, for loving. Many times the young are our greatest teachers.

. . . .

CHAPTER SIX

Our Lady of Czestochowa

The image of Our Lady of Czestochowa is believed to have been painted by St. Luke the evangelist on a tabletop made by Jesus. Brought from Jerusalem, the icon was discovered by the Emperor Constantine's mother and given a place of honor in Constantinople for hundreds of years. In the year 803, the image was given to a Greek princess as a wedding gift and enshrined in the royal palace of Belz. When the town was incorporated into the Polish kingdom, the painting was brought to Poland and placed in the monastery of Jasna Gora in 1382.

During a Hussite invasion, the painting was stolen, but the horses pulling the wagon containing the painting refused to move. The image was thrown down in the mud, and Our Lady's face was slashed.

Although the painting was cleaned and attempts were made to repair the damage, the slash marks remain on her face today.

In 1655, Swedish troops ready to attack Czestochowa miraculously retreated as Polish soldiers prayed before the icon of Our Lady. And in 1920, as the Soviet army gathered on the banks of the Vistula River, soldiers and citizens prayed to Our Lady, and she appeared in the clouds above Warsaw. The Russians were defeated, and once again the Queen and Protector of Poland prevailed for her people. In 1945, half a million people made the pilgrimage to Czestochowa in thanksgiving to Our Lady. Pope John Paul II visited the shrine in 1979, 1983, 1991, and 1997.

. . . .

National Shrine of Our Lady of Czestochowa
DOYLESTOWN, PENNSYLVANIA

More than once we think our GPS is guiding us in the wrong direction, but suddenly, as we round a hill, we can see the entrance. As we drive up the hill, the houses shrink out of sight, and all we can see is the shrine, surrounded by rolling hills and trees, as if it were all there is in the town.

We arrive late, and as we enter a side door, hungry and thirsty after going without lunch, we find the cafeteria and ask a man mopping there where we can find food. He says in somewhat broken English with a heavy Polish accent, "Not today. I cook for you on Sunday. Come back on Sunday." We thank him and move toward the door, but he begins shouting, "Lady! Lady!" For a split second, we expect an exception on a meal, until he points and continues, "The church!" We look, as again we thank him and move toward the object of his plea.

On the way, we are drawn to the outdoor side alcove where a grotto has been formed in the wall. Our Lady of Lourdes and Bernadette are present, and there are spouts where we can fill our holy water bottles. Rosaries and scapulars hang all over the stones and the images—gifts left in thanksgiving for answered prayers. The site is powerful, and as we get closer we can see hundreds of small pieces of folded paper tucked into the rock surrounding Our Lady. A sea of petitions are jammed into the tight spaces, begging relief from the sufferings of this life.

We enter the lower level of the church first and visit at the altars of the Our Lady of Guadalupe, Divine Mercy, and Mary of Nazareth chapels. Each chapel is as beautiful as the next, and their walls tell the stories and allow us to enter into the devotion. Entering the chapel of Our Lady of Czestochowa, we join others in adoration of the exposed Blessed Sacrament. Again, how fortunate we are to be led to Christ. The reverence in this place is a reminder that the journey is much more than travels through the countryside and snapshots of pictures. The journey of visiting Our Lady brings us to these graces that lay waiting for us to receive. Here her Son waits.

The interior of the main church tells the story of Christianity in Poland and the history of America in the bright, colorful stained-glass windows. Stretched above the main altar is a sixty-five-foot relief of the Trinity, with the image of Our Lady of Czestochowa inserted amid huge trumpeting angels. We read the explanation that tells of Mary's tie to the mystery of the Trinity and her share in the mission of giving the grace that leads us to her Son, who leads us to the Father and the Holy Spirit. The picture was blessed by Pope John XXIII in 1962 and traveled around the U.S. before being enshrined for the dedication of the new shrine here in 1966.

We visit St. Anne's Chapel and several other areas of devotion before walking through the outdoor Stations of the Cross and the Rosary Garden. We are about to leave when we spot the red barn at the back of the cemetery. As we enter what turns out to be the first chapel, the original shrine, we are once again offered an opportunity for a moment with Our Lady. Father Michael Zembrzuski, a Pauline monk from Poland, converted this barn into a chapel and dedicated it to Our Lady of Czestochowa in 1955. After traveling as a missionary for three years, Fr. Michael saw the need to build a shrine that would both strengthen the spirit of the Polish immigrants and share the Polish tradition and culture.

As we kneel before Our Lady, we too are strengthened. From the time we enter the cafeteria and venture through the church, the chapel, at the altars, in the gift shop, and around the grounds to our final visit here in the original chapel, we can feel the spirit of the Polish community. Their authentic love and dedication to Our Lady and to those of us who take the time to visit touches something deep inside us. Standing in front of the huge statue of Pope John Paul II with his arms outstretched and reading *"Otworzcie Szeroko Drzwi Chrystusowi"*—"Open Wide the Doors to Christ"—we know that we are not just welcome but that all are welcome, all are invited, and in turn, all will receive the gift of Our Lady's protection, the gift of strength for the daily battles of life.

. . . .

Black Madonna Shrine and Grottos
Eureka, Missouri

The temperature has to be close to one hundred degrees. The place is unattended for a reason. It is just too hot to be wandering around the back roads of Missouri, but we persevere. We show up—and we are the only ones. The large concrete slab with the metal roof is filled with pews, and the open-air Chapel of the Hills contains an altar with statues and a large image of Our Lady of Czestochowa. The chapel was built in the 1960s to replace the original cedar chapel that was built by Brother Bronislaus Luszcz in the late 1930s and was later destroyed by an arsonist.

A group of Franciscan Brothers were invited by the archbishop of St. Louis to come from Poland and build a nursing home for men. Br. Bronislaus came, bringing with him the memories of the people of Poland making long pilgrimages to Our Lady to her shrine in Jasna Gora. He wanted us to share his love for Our Lady. He cleared the land and built the chapel and all of the grottos to offer pilgrims a place to rest in the arms of Our Mother.

We take a small pamphlet and begin our self-guided walking tour. The area outside the open chapel is a semicircle of rock grottos, and the first one we come to is of Our Lady of Fatima. We move on to Our Lady of Perpetual Help, which marks the place where Br. Bronislaus died of heatstroke. We take a few minutes to talk about this man who dedicated his time and his talent to bring Our Lady to the people who come to visit. We can hardly stand the heat as we walk the grounds and cannot imagine working in it.

The Crucifixion Grotto is high on the hill, and we read that it was once a point of reference for hikers in the woods during winter. We check out the jewels and the seashells and small statues and birds worked into the rocks. A pathway leads around the side to a large natural grotto containing a nativity scene. As we venture up the hill behind a scene of the crucifixion, we find a statue of Mary holding the infant Jesus, with water trickling down at the base into a fishpond. The area is peaceful, and we read, "Mary Mother, through my pain and fear, show me the loving way." We love this spot, and the kids love seeing the fish and putting their hands in the cool water coming down off the hill.

The short walk back to the chapel area brings us back into the full brunt of the heat. We take a little more time near the altar, noticing for the first time that the candles are lit, the holy water container is full, and there is a cooler of ice-cold drinking water. Someone has been here. Someone has prepared a place in the stillness. There is more here than we realize. There is beauty and comfort. The light of Christ burns in a place that at first glance seems deserted. There is no one here to thank, no one to talk to, no gifts to buy. But there is love.

We cannot leave without going around the drive to see what else is on the property. We find a field across from what used to be the nursing home with the remains of a Lourdes Grotto. I once read—and I truly believe—that there is nothing that has at one time honored Our Lady that does not still bring peace. I close my eyes and imagine the water flowing through the grotto. I imagine people standing in the field as Mass is prayed at the altar. They have come to visit family in the nursing home, the Franciscan Brothers, Our Lady. I ask my son what he thinks about this place. I ask him why this man, these brothers, would come from Poland and build this place, literally in exchange for their lives. He simply says, "You know why. For God. They do it all for the love of God. It's all about him. You know that."

. . . .

Prayer

Mary, you lead us to these places where the people are authentic. They speak the language of their country and live in community with one another. Teach us to be authentic in our love for your Son. Draw us closer to him and help us to duplicate our love for him. These people are real and true. Help us to be the same.

.   .   .   .

Grace

Our Lady worked behind the scenes in the name of her Son. She wants us, too, to work for him when no one is watching. She wants us to visit, though there are no witnesses. She wants us to pray, though no one sees. During the times in our lives when we may feel beaten down and worn out, she is with us, quenching our thirst, cooling us down, and keeping the flame alive, all for God.

CHAPTER SEVEN

.   .   .   .

Immaculate Conception

The Immaculate Conception of Mary was declared a dogma of the Catholic Church in 1854 by Pope Pius IX in the apostolic constitution *Ineffabilis Deus*. This teaching states that Mary was born free from sin, even original sin. From the moment of her conception, Mary was redeemed and received God's grace in anticipation of her role as the Mother of our Savior. God told the serpent in Genesis 3:15, "I will put enmity between you and the woman, between your seed and her seed." Mary would never be under the power of sin but would be always in a state of grace. She was born pure, as an expression of God's love and to bring Christ into the world.

In 1792, John Carroll, the first bishop of the United States, placed our country under the protection of the Immaculate Conception. Pope Pius chose her to be patroness of the United States in 1847. Mary, keep us safe in your mantle.

.   .   .   .

Basilica of the National Shrine of the Immaculate Conception
WASHINGTON, D.C.

In this enormous national shrine, it is easy to get lost in the splendor of all that surrounds us, in the history of the building and the materials: the brick and mortar, the clay, the glazes, and the stone mosaics. It is easy to get caught up in the grandeur, the donors, and the visuals. But what lies deep in the recesses of all that surrounds us is the heart of our faith. Within each alcove rests Our Lady, open to the visitors, waiting for the multicultural arrivals. She is here to bring us to her Son. She speaks every language, and she beckons us to visit her Son in the Blessed Sacrament. She calls us to cleanse ourselves in the renewal of the sacrament of reconciliation. She, as our Mother, and all of us are here to bring together a world. Here there are no barriers that cannot be worked through, no one held back because of race or nation; there are no foreigners.

We spend hours visiting the largest Catholic church in the United States. We move one by one through the seventy chapels dedicated to Our Lady, spending time reading and praying and learning more about those who have gone before us, about people who have come in faith from other countries to this land of freedom. We learn of Mary's protection and love for all people.

In 1910, Bishop Thomas Shahan, the rector of Catholic University of America, suggested building the shrine to honor Mary as the Immaculate Conception, patroness of the United States. Pope Pius X not only supported the idea but also personally contributed to the project. As we stand in the magnificent Upper Church, we can only imagine the impact this shrine made upon those who planned it, those who built it, and now those who visit it. The walls, archways, and doors tell the history of the Church. We watch as families and individuals take time at certain special devotion areas. They walk and they touch the statues, running their hands over the words. They kneel and they pray. The workmen are moving quietly throughout the chapels, replacing empty candleholders with fresh opportunities for petitions to be lifted up to heaven.

The mosaics of Our Lady of Perpetual Help, the Assumption, and the Immaculate Conception make us stop and admire the art, the time spent on each piece for the Mother of Jesus. The mosaics of Our Lady of Guadalupe make us feel part of a grand procession. All the work has been done to make this shrine a place of prayer, a holy place, a comfortable place for people of all nationalities.

As we move to the crypt level, we pass a beautiful image of the holy family at rest during the flight into Egypt. Mary and the child Jesus are the focal point propped in the middle, exhausted from the journey, with Joseph curled up on one side and the donkey on the other. We have journeyed, and we find this place, this shrine, to rest, to give it all up as a family. In the Lower Chapel, we are not surprised to happen upon exposition of the Blessed Sacrament. Mary leads us to the beauty of this Church, amongst the saints and the angels, to rest before her Son.

We begin taking time to go from chapel to chapel, kneeling and saying the prayers we find at the kneelers and around the walls. The messages are pertinent for today. In this one place, we join in a pilgrimage to shrines all over the world.

The Venetian glass mosaic of Mary, Queen of Missions, tells of the missionary work done by the Oblates of Mary Immaculate. They evangelize all over the world, and in this chapel we hear the call to work bringing others to Christ right in our own neighborhoods.

The bright gold of Our Lady of La Vang lures us to learn more of her story. In 1798, amid bitter persecution in Vietnam, many Catholics fled to the jungle for safety. They suffered from cold and sickness and hunger. At night, they gathered at the foot of a great tree to pray the rosary. One night the Blessed Mother, holding the child Jesus, appeared and comforted the people, telling them to boil the leaves from the trees to cure the sick. Mary appeared many times offering comfort and encouragement. As we stand in her midst, she is our refuge. She understands hardships. She has compassion. She consoles.

Devotion to Our Lady of Mariazell comes from Austria, where a monk's journey was blocked by a boulder, until a statue of Our Lady was set upon it and the rock split in half. The monk built a cell and remained in prayer. The cell grew into a monastery and is now a chapel where the miraculous statue rests upon the site of the first cell. Mary helps us to break the barriers that prevent us from reaching our goals and God's will for us.

The chapels are filled with beautiful statues or images of Our Lady from different countries around the world. The saints related to the countries are often represented in the chapel, either by a statue or a quote. Each sacred place has an offering of grace from Our Lady. As we visit, we feel like each chapel and the message inside is the most important one that Mary would like us to take with us from this journey. We have truly visited shrines from all over the world.

· ·

Prayer

Mary, Mother of all Nations, help us to live as one in peace. Give us the grace we need to go out and to spread truth. Give us the grace to spread the love of your Son. In this massive place, we find hope. Help us to frequent the sacrament of reconciliation so we may be more like you, pure and holy.

· ·

Grace

There are many graces in this basilica for all who enter. Take the time in each individual chapel to learn more about different cultures. Visit in the same place as Pope John Paul II and Pope Benedict. In a city where there is much to do, Mary is glad we have chosen to visit her first, just as so many before us have.

CHAPTER EIGHT

· ·

The Assumption of Mary

. . . .

The Assumption of Mary was declared a dogma of the Catholic Church in 1950 by Pope Pius XII, with the apostolic constitution *Munificentissimus Deus.* This teaching states that Mary was taken body and soul into heaven. In the *Catechism of the Catholic Church,* we read, "Finally the Immaculate Virgin, preserved free from all stain of original sin, when the course of her earthly life was finished, was taken up body and soul into heavenly glory, and exalted by the Lord as Queen over all things, so that she might be the more fully conformed to her Son, the Lord of lords and conqueror of sin and death."[3] The Feast of the Assumption of Mary, August 15, is a holy day of obligation.

. . . .

Basilica of the National Shrine of the Assumption of the Blessed Virgin Mary

BALTIMORE, MARYLAND

Upon entering the Baltimore basilica, the first Catholic cathedral built in the United States, we are offered a tour. Benjamin Henry Latrobe, the same architect chosen to work on the basilica, also worked on the U.S. Capitol. The style is much the same, with open, clear windows and large domes. The light colors and twenty-four skylights from the center dome make the church seem fresh and spacious. The dome above the main altar depicts the assumption of Mary, while multiple archways lead to different areas of devotion, each filled with history and beauty.

Bishop John Carroll came from France as the first bishop in the United States. Provincial Councils of Baltimore were held in the nineteenth century, establishing parish and parochial school systems and compiling the *Baltimore Catechism* so faith teaching could be consistent throughout the dioceses. We ask about the hat hanging from the ceiling, and our guide explains that the *galero*, the red cardinal's hat, is hung from the ceiling of a cardinal's home cathedral when he dies. When the hat disintegrates and falls to the floor, it is believed that the cardinal's soul has been received into heaven. This particular *galero* has long since disintegrated and is tucked inside the newer one we see hanging. This practice stopped in 1969. The inside of the basilica has been changed many times, following the tastes of the different pastors. The skylights have been covered and the colors changed to red and gold. For the two-hundred-year anniversary, the interior was restored to its original appearance.

Our guide takes us down below the basilica to the crypt where they have recently shoveled out the basement, bricked the floor, and built Our Lady Seat of Wisdom chapel. This was the original intent of the architect Latrobe. Once again, it is in this small place that we find peace. The archways are all brick, and the girls walk through to see the shrines set up in the arched, grotto-like areas. There are small rooms filled with the history of the Church and of America. Many famous people have journeyed through this monument of faith, including Blessed Mother Teresa, President Andrew Johnson, Ralph Waldo Emerson, and John Paul II. The self-guided tour would have never given us this kind of information, and we are grateful for the knowledge and insight of our guide.

. . . .

Prayer

Mary, you reign in heaven body and soul as queen. In your basilica, we learn the history of the Catholic Church in America. Teach us to be proud of our heritage. This basilica sent out many good men; may we too go out and proclaim the Good News to all we meet. In deed and in action, greatness reigns. May we remember our roots, be clear and fresh in our faith, and help to bring others closer to our heavenly rewards.

. . . .

Grace

Together, we learn the beginnings of our Church. We better understand the roots of our faith, as we are able to connect with many of the other places we have visited and the people whose names we have heard. We realize that we are standing in the place where the bishops from Europe met and put together the *Catechism* so that we can all be united in our dioceses. It is this connection, this sense of belonging together that gives us strength and unity.

CHAPTER NINE

. . . .

Our Lady of Consolation

In the seventeenth century, Father James Brocquart and students from
the Jesuit College in Luxembourg, as an act of honor and devotion,
began processing a statue of Our Lady through the streets, placing her
beneath a cross near the outside walls of the city. Fr. Brocquart began
construction on a chapel the following year on that same spot, but a
plague hit Luxembourg and construction stopped after Fr. Brocquart
became seriously ill to the point of death. He prayed to Our Lady
and vowed to finish the chapel if he lived. Miraculously, Fr. Brocquart
recovered and completed the chapel—and people began flocking to
Our Lady for her help and her intercession.

In 1666, the city publicly made Mary their patroness under the title, Mary, Mother of God, Consoler of the Afflicted. During the French Revolution, the small, old chapel was completely destroyed and the statue was taken to the Church of the Immaculate Conception, today's cathedral in Luxembourg. The church has been enlarged and renovated to accommodate the large number of pilgrims who journey there each year.

. . . .

Basilica and National Shrine of Our Lady of Consolation
CAREY, OHIO

Stories of miracles pique our curiosity. All of us would like visual images to confirm the stories and help us believe in the miracles. We travel so we can see, so we can touch, so we can understand, so we too may be healed, strengthened, and consoled.

From the direction of our travels, we have a difficult time finding a hotel. With the sun gone, the long stretches of countryside make for a dark and somewhat tedious drive. What would probably be beautiful in the day is lost in the darkness. We finally find a place to rest, and we enter the next morning somewhat refreshed and curious. We drive more, searching for the easiest passage so that we will be on time for Mass. As we come into the city, we feel ourselves change, and our stress to get somewhere begins to give way to calmness. We find the Shrine of Our Lady of Consolation inside the basilica we have come to for Mass.

The statue of Our Lady there—made at the request of Father Joseph Peter Gloden to be as close to the original statue as possible—was brought from Luxembourg in 1875. Fr. Gloden was the pastor in Frenchtown, Ohio, assigned to what was then named St. Edward Church in Carey. He visited the community once a week, saying Mass, teaching religion, and working on the unfinished church. Father asked the parishioners to pray to Mary under the title of Our Lady of Consolation. When he was in seminary, he was stricken with typhoid and nearly died. He promised Our Lady that if he lived, he would name the first church he could in honor of her.

When the statue arrived in Frenchtown, Our Lady was to be processed through the streets and presented to the new church in Carey. A terrible storm began the night before, threatening the plans for the procession, but parishioners still showed up at the church early the next morning with umbrellas, ready to brave the rain. As soon as the statue of Our Lady was brought from inside the church, the sun shone over the entire procession line. Rain could be seen pouring down on both sides of the lines of people, but not a drop fell on anyone in the procession. As soon as Our Lady reached the church in Carey and entered, the rain drenched all who remained outside. The first miracle of Our Lady of Consolation had occurred, and many more would follow.

As Mass ends, we are instructed to take some time in the lower church and see the many offerings left for Our Lady in thanksgiving for the miracles, comfort, and love. After enjoying the beautiful stained-glass windows and the image of Mary crowned and holding a scepter, presenting her Son to the world, as well as the beautiful image of the Sorrowful Mother on the opposite altar, we venture down below the church.

We find it difficult to believe the cabinets upon cabinets, with rows upon rows of dresses made for Our Lady of Consolation in thanksgiving for answered prayers. Cabinets filled with braces and crutches and letters and liquor bottles and photos, all left at the altar of Our Lady as that visual image, that sign of gratitude, of thanksgiving and faith. Here we get that same feeling that we should leave something in gratitude to Our Lady. We take time.

We visit the first church across the street from the basilica, which was quickly outgrown after word of miracles began and pilgrimages increased. Again, we take time. We visit the beautiful Shrine Park, following the Stations of the Cross and pausing at the large dome with the statue of Mary on top. We picture the procession coming from the basilica on the Feast of the Assumption, just as so many processed on the day they brought the statue from Frenchtown to Carey.

We take time in exchange for the gift of this place that reminds us that Our Lady is here to console us in our time of sorrow, to relieve us in our time of trouble, and to intercede for us in our needs. At the cross, she experienced deep sorrow, and she wants to protect us from that kind of misery. She overwhelms us with the tangible, the believable, and the amazing, and she gives us the grace to acknowledge our troubles and our fears and leave them at the altar.

. . . .

Prayer

Mary, console us in our times of fear and hurt and sadness. Ask your Son to heal us of what keeps us from fully giving ourselves to him spiritually, physically, and mentally. As we see all that others have left at the altar, help us to recognize all we should leave, as well. And as you relieve us from the burdens of this life, may we return to you in thanksgiving, always acknowledging, always grateful.

. . . .

Grace

In a world that often frowns upon imperfection, we find a place to be open and honest about all our fears and our cares and our sorrows. We find in Our Lady a place to be healed and to be loved. We find at the base of the altar a place to leave behind all our flaws, all our failings. We slow down. We take time, and we find our Mother waiting to take to her Son all our needs and in return to give us the grace to take him to an imperfect, suffering world.

CHAPTER TEN

. . . .

Our Lady of Sorrows

· ·

Early in the thirteenth century, seven young men left Florence and formed a community at Mt. Senario, Italy. On Good Friday, 1239, Mary appeared to the men and asked them to form an order, specifically to promote devotion to her sufferings. They founded the Servants of Mary (Servite Order), vesting themselves in a black habit, taking vows of poverty, chastity, and obedience, and following the Rule of St. Augustine.

The Seven Sorrows Rosary, or Seven Dolours, is one of their devotions, which is used to meditate on events in the life of Mary: the prophecy of Simeon, the flight into Egypt, the loss of the child Jesus for three days, meeting Jesus on the way to Calvary, the crucifixion and death of Jesus, Jesus taken from the cross and put in the arms of Mary, and the burial of Jesus.

Our Lady of Sorrows is portrayed in different ways in art. There are paintings, such as the *Mater Dolorosa* and the *Stabat Mater*. There are statues, such as *Our Lady of the Seven Sorrows*, in which Mary is portrayed with seven swords through her heart, and the *Pietá*, where Jesus lies across the lap of his Mother after his crucifixion.

. . . .

Our Lady of Sorrows Basilica
CHICAGO, ILLINOIS

Work can keep us from many blessings in our lives. We do not mean to get so busy, but we do. Whether we work in the home or outside the home, life keeps us on the run. We have to make special efforts to escape. We have to just drop what we are doing, despite what others may think or say, and take the time not to miss the opportunities.

Going to Chicago for work has been a part of our routine for thirty years. Fly up. Take care of business. Fly home. Simple. Then, I look up the possibility of making a few shrine visits, and we drive. I leave the work to the others for a few hours, and I take the time to visit. I cannot believe how close this basilica is to where I have had meetings for years. I've just never taken the time.

Today I drive about twenty minutes, maybe less, to this beautiful church, which also contains the National Shrine of St. Peregrine. With all the people touched by cancer who have asked for prayers, I am overwhelmed by the opportunity to include their names in the book of intentions. St. Peregrine was a brother of the Servants of Mary (Servites).

As I wander, I notice two sisters who walk around the basilica and a priest in the back, kneeling in prayer. I think they are with the monastery, but after talking with them, I discover that the two sisters are there on mission, selling rosaries from their convent in Mexico. The priest is from another parish in Chicago and is just taking them around the city. They are headed to the zoo. I am thankful for the chance to participate in their mission. They are trying to increase their numbers because there is so much work to do. I certainly agree.

Pope Pius XII raised this church to a basilica in 1956. He referred to the church as one of the most important shrines dedicated to spreading devotion to Our Sorrowful Mother. Since 1937, the Sorrowful Mother Novena has spread to two thousand other churches and chapels. The altars dedicated to Our Lady are breathtaking in their marble work and painting. One of the most striking altars depicts Our Lady asking the seven founders of the Servite Order to promote devotion to her sufferings. She stands, arms open, with angels and cherubs surrounding her. I cannot imagine anyone refusing her request. The altar of Our Lady of Fatima shows her heart encircled by a crown of thorns. The three peasant children kneel on the floor in front. The Our Lady of Sorrows altar shows Mary with hands clenched, her eyes down and her veil large enough to keep her face in the shadow.

Walking to the back, I find the chapel where a replica of Michelangelo's *Pietá* has taken the place of the old baptistry. I kneel, and I am so close I can see how young this mother is who holds her Son's body. Her lap is oversized, and I realize that she has enough room not just for her Son but for all of our sorrows. Her lap is large enough for me to crawl up into and be comforted. I can feel myself want to cry. This young mother, younger than I am, is willing to take on my sorrows along with her own. And I allow it. The loss of siblings and of friends and of grandparents, the fear, anxiety, and worry are all taken from me here in the corner of this huge basilica. I want to stay, but it is time.

. . . .

Sorrowful Mother Shrine
BELLEVUE, OHIO

Mary loves our best efforts. She knows we have flaws. Not every attempt will be perfect, and some may not be complete, but when we try, when we do all we can do, the rewards are great.

My husband and I push ourselves to get from one place to the next. The long drive is beautiful, and spending time together, just the two of us, can be a blessing in itself. But we arrive too late. The church and the gift shop are closed. It is cold and rainy, and we are tempted to turn around and leave. But we have traveled far to this pilgrimage site. The site is the oldest in the Midwest, started in 1850 and run by the missionary priests of the Most Precious Blood dedicated to Our Lady. So we stay, like so many before us, and we walk over to the large outdoor Pietá Chapel.

With the increasing number of people visiting the shrine, the Pietá Chapel was built and dedicated in 1968. We see from this large plat-form another shrine, where the Madonna of the Precious Blood is holding the child Jesus and offering the cup to St. Gaspar del Bufalo, the founder the Missionaries of the Precious Blood. As we leave, we notice a wide path covered by leaves. We are not sure where it leads, but we can see a building at the end of the path and know there is some-thing more, so we go forth, despite the growing darkness. Reaching the end of the path, we discover a Mexican-style building with Our Lady of Guadalupe inside, and from there we can see it all. We can see the reason we have come and the reason we have stayed.

There are shrines all through the woods made of different materials to coordinate with the heritage of the figure. Suddenly, lights come on and we can find our way, despite the fallen leaves. Grottos of St. Francis; St. Catherine of Siena; St. Teresa; Mother Teresa; St. Jude; St. Anthony; Our Lady of Mount Carmel; Mary Queen of Martyrs; Our Lady of Fatima; St. Kateri; the Agony in the Garden; Our Lady of Czestochowa; St. Faustina; the Sacred Heart; the Holy Family; Tomb of Christ; Our Lady of Lourdes; and more are sprinkled through the woods. The area is definitely set to do exactly what it was built for: to foster devotion to our Lady and to provide a peaceful setting for prayer and reflection. We actually enjoy being alone.

Before we drive off, we witness another couple. They have come to pray together at the shrine, to visit the grottos, and to walk together in peace. They have come to offer devotion to Our Lady, and they, too, are a little too late and yet, right on time.

· ·

Prayer

Mary, Sorrowful Mother, you wait as we make our best efforts, and you hold a place for us. With your arms wide open, you welcome our sorrows and our joys, our need for comfort and healing. You give us what we need because we have journeyed to you. We have taken the time, and you give us space. You offer a place, and in you we find peace. Mary, intercede for us with your Son.

· ·

Grace

We can often see more than we have ever seen and understand messages when we take the time alone. Left alone, we take time. Left alone, we experience differently. Left alone, we are filled. Venturing out on one's own, we are rewarded. Some days, Mary wants us one-on-one.

. . . .

Our Lady of Charity

In 1612, three young men went out in their boat to the Bay of Nipe in Cuba for salt. A raging storm threatened their lives, and they turned to Mary in prayer. The winds calmed, and the clouds cleared. The three young men then found a board floating on the water carrying a statue of Mary holding the child Jesus. They noticed that, despite the storm, it was completely dry. The small board had the inscription, "I am the Virgin of Charity." They took the statue to the nearest village, Barajaguas, and it was given a place of honor in the church.

The people noticed that the statue would often disappear, so they moved it to a church in El Cobre, but it disappeared from there also. A young girl named Apolonia reported seeing Our Lady in the mountains of El Cobre. After a few other such events, the decision was made to build a chapel, now known as the National Shrine of Our Lady of Charity, to Our Lady in the mountains. In 1916, Pope Benedict XV made Our Lady of Charity "Patroness of Cuba."

.   .   .   .

National Shrine of Our Lady of Charity
MIAMI, FLORIDA

The waves are splashing up against the wall surrounding the shrine. The ground is soggy, as if the water has been over the seawall recently. We are standing at rough waters that lead from Miami, Florida, all the way to Cuba. We are standing at the end of the route that brought the image of Our Lady of Charity from Cuba along with thousands fleeing a Marxist regime that tried to impose atheism upon the people. When Archbishop Coleman F. Carroll celebrated the first Mass on September 8, 1961, the Feast of Our Lady of Charity, he was surprised at the arrival of nearly thirty thousand exiles. Our Lady unites them to one another and to their homeland.

As we enter the shrine, we see the 747-square-foot mural that covers the entire wall behind the altar. The artist painted Our Lady in the middle and began with Christ in her arms but left him unfinished until the very end. He wanted to emphasize that Mary leads us to Christ, who is the beginning and the end, the alpha and the omega. Just as Jesus calmed the sea for the apostles, he is here for all people from every country during the roughest times. Sixty-three figures tell the history of the Cuban people. Beginning with Christopher Columbus, Our Lady of Charity, the Franciscan Fathers, generals, teachers, popes, priests, and bishops, the mural captures those who worked for freedom, taught the faith, and loved the people.

As we go behind the shrine to the Eucharistic chapel, we notice the beauty of the monstrance that holds Our Lord. Directly behind the monstrance, the wall is filled by a huge stained-glass image of Our Lady of Charity in mostly light blues. My daughter walks right down front and kneels close to Jesus. The water from the ocean can be seen through the stained glass and reminds us of the statue of Our Lady drifting on a board, waiting to be pulled from the rocky waters. Mary waits, completely untouched by the storms. She wants us to visit with her because she has unconditional love to give. She wants to help us, to smooth the rough places in our lives.

As we leave the chapel, we sit once again in front of the mural along with many others who have come to visit the shrine. The image of Our Lady of Charity, with her gold-adorned dress and crown, glows behind the altar. She is the little piece of Cuba they have brought with them as they left their homes and their traditions.

There is reverence and respect shown by all who come and go. A line forms for confessions, and there is a consistent flow. They come to remember those who have come before them, those who built the shrine with their own donations, to leave this legacy for their children. They come to honor the place built so they could gather as one. We sit with Our Lady who gives hope, who gives protection, who gives love. We sit, and we are grateful for our faith.

. . . .

Prayer

Mary, protector of us all, we pray for our country of many cultures. We pray that, as we live together and learn from one another, we will become one in your Son. You lead us to him who saves and you protect us from the storms of this life. Help us to work as one for peace in our countries, to live in one faith, and to pass the truth on to our families. Help us to be examples of charity to our families and to one another.

. . . .

Grace

There are many places in America where it may not seem like we are in the United States. But, when we pray together, when we come together to bring glory to God, when we walk right down front and kneel close, we are all one. The languages mix together in perfect harmony, and we are heard as one group of children. Mary brings us together in charity and love and leads us to her Son.

CHAPTER TWELVE

. . . .

Mary, Queen of the Universe

Queen of the Universe is one of the many titles for the Mother of Jesus. Pope Pius XII wrote an entire encyclical in 1954, *Ad Caeli Reginam*, proclaiming Mary as Queen. With references to and quotes from the Bible and the writings of the Church Fathers and theologians, Pope Pius XII explained that we should revere Mary as Queen not just because of all this evidence, but because she shared in the role of our redemption with Christ the King. He established the Feast of Mary's Queenship as May 31, praying that her grace and mercy would bring peace to our world.

Ten years later, Pope Paul IV, in the Dogmatic Constitution on the Church, *Lumen Gentium*, stated, "Finally, the Immaculate Virgin, preserved free from all guilt of original sin, on the completion of her earthly sojourn, was taken up body and soul into heavenly glory, and exalted by the Lord as Queen of the universe, that she might be the more fully conformed to her Son, the Lord of lords and the conqueror of sin and death" (59).

Mary as Queen of the Universe, taken body and soul to heaven, reigns there as our protector and as our hope. She is waiting to shower down the graces given to her to give to those who ask for them. She will bring peace to our universe. May we imitate her love and her kindness and live as one.

. . . .

Basilica of the National Shrine of Mary, Queen of the Universe
ORLANDO, FLORIDA

Crowds, traffic, and noise obviously can make us believe that there is no place for a peaceful moment in this world. We are easily distracted by our busy surroundings, and marketers pay a lot of money to keep us looking for the hoopla. But today, we find a place where Jesus dwells and where Our Lady has been waiting.

Signs for outlet malls, hotel deals, and Disney World attract and excite us. We would love to spend the weekend shopping and riding the latest rides. But, we have pulled out of traffic for a completely different reason, and we find many others who have done the same. My children had come to Disney World the previous summer and attended Mass at Mary, Queen of the Universe, bringing home brochures and telling me all about the basilica. Decades earlier, they would have celebrated Mass in their hotel. Due to the number of tourists coming to Orlando back in the 1970s, the diocese of Orlando arranged to celebrate Mass in area hotels. Father F. Joseph Harte was in charge of arranging the Mass schedules. When the projection for visitors rose to thirty million per year, he and Bishop Thomas Grady realized the need for a permanent facility to shepherd the faithful. And the end result, opening in 1993, is so much more.

The rose window and the holy water font with the two thirty-foot archways at the entrance of the basilica are magnificent. We choose first to spend time in the Day Chapel, where a mosaic of Our Lady of Guadalupe has captured my time and attention. A special place has been made for the Patroness of the Americas here within the Shrine of the Universe. The intricate detail of the mosaic, the blue colors, and the beautiful stained-glass replica of the midnight sky recreate the splendor of the universe. We kneel and pray to Our Lady.

The first noticeable image inside the church is the corpus of Christ, the image of sacrifice and love, suspended above the altar backed by a crystal cross. As we walk closer, we find the statue of Our Lady of the Universe. She is pure white. The child Jesus has his head resting upon her with a slight smile on his face. We immediately feel at peace here. We feel at home. From the turbulent outside world, we have found a place apart. Directly behind the altar is the adoration chapel. We kneel and pray and take a moment to be grateful for God's presence.

As we wander outside, my youngest and I are drawn to the Mother and Child Outdoor Chapel. There are a mom and daughter there with a child in a stroller. Obviously they are in prayer, holding on to one another and the child. Here, the bronze sculpture depicts Mary leaning over to embrace her Son. We are still, capturing the tender moments.

The Rosary Garden contains a bronze bust of Pope John Paul II, with the words from his apostolic letter *Rosarium Virginis Mariae,* "To recite the rosary is nothing other than to *contemplate with Mary the face of Christ*" (3). As we walk around the paths, we can see coming toward us two very excited young women and their mother. They cannot wait to get to the garden. Both girls are holding their journals, and both love moving their fingers over the words and the raised rosary on the bronze bust of Pope John Paul II. We look at one another, and our faces light up seeing their excitement to spend time with Our Lady. We truly witness the face of Christ.

. . . .

Prayer

Mary, Our Queen, teach us daily to pull away from the traffic of our lives and spend time with your Son. We live in a hectic world. Our minds never seem to rest. Help us to take the tender moments and to contemplate with you the face of Christ.

. . . .

Grace

In this big world, this universe, there are places that give peace, that help us to witness to something so much more. Today, you grace us with witnessing to your Son in one another.

CHAPTER THIRTEEN

. . . .

Our Lady of La Leche

In 1598, an image of the Blessed Virgin Mary breastfeeding the Baby Jesus was rescued in Spain from a place it had no reason to be in and put in the home of a married couple who were expecting their first child. The mother was suffering from a serious illness, and she and the baby were not expected to live. The couple prayed before Our Lady continuously for a safe delivery and for the life of their unborn child. The wife was miraculously cured of her illness and delivered a healthy baby. News spread quickly about the healing, and many came to pray to Our Lady for their families.

When King Philip III heard the news of Mary's intercession, he had the image placed in the shrine he built in honor of Nuestra Señora de la Leche y Buen Parto. As people visited the shrine to pray, stories spread of healings, good fortune, and miracles. Devotion to Our Lady of La Leche spread throughout Spain.

. . . .

Shrine of Our Lady of La Leche
ST. AUGUSTINE, FLORIDA

Many events in our lives can bring us to our knees. Requests for a safe arrival, a healing, or even a miracle bring us to prayer, to a cry for help, for intercession, and for guidance.

We normally travel without hotel reservations because it's fun to feel what it's like to have the adventure of not knowing. It is often exciting to see where Our Lady leads us. This journey to St. Augustine during spring break almost left us with no room in the inn. We have heard that phrase many times, but this night, we have no idea that the Eighteenth Annual Rhythm and Ribs Festival and the five-hundredth anniversary of Ponce de Leon's discovery of Florida are happening. Thousands of people have settled in for a weekend of live music, games, and award-winning barbeque along with a celebration of history. We are given literally one of the last rooms in the city. This night, we feel blessed once again.

In 1565, as Pedro Menendez de Aviles battled rough waters and torrential storms sailing from Spain to Florida, Father Francisco Lopez de Mendoza prayed for their safe arrival. Others on board visited him for confession in fear they might lose their lives. As several men and three priests deserted the mission at their stop in Puerto Rico, the others forged on through raging seas to claim the land and bring Christianity to America. As they touched land, Pedro Menendez knelt and kissed the cross held by Fr. Lopez, as did the others when they disembarked.

A bronze statue of Fr. Francisco Lopez de Mendoza commemorates the place of the first Mass celebrated, and a cross stands 208 feet tall, summoning us and others to see and learn the history of our faith. In the early seventeenth century, Franciscan missionaries brought the devotion of Our Lady of La Leche from Spain to the chapel at Mission Nombre de Dios. We read that this is the first Marian shrine in America. As we visit the chapel, the fourth since the original due to wars and storms, we feel a sense of its mission, a place built to teach Christianity.

The style of the chapel is simple and rustic, and it is a place for time between Our Lady and her children with their needs, their requests, and their gratitude. Outside the chapel, there are Stations of the Cross, meditations on the seven sorrows of Mary, and several smaller shrines to Our Lady, including the *Pietá*, Our Lady of Guadalupe, and Our Lady of Perpetual Help. The beautiful weather allows us to take time at all the areas.

Before leaving, we head to the museum, which is filled with the history of St. Augustine. A young man greets us, eager for us to watch the short movie and to learn more about the area. I ask about the devotion to Our Lady of La Leche, wanting to know more about her visitors. One of the Sisters of St. Joseph is kind enough to spend time with us, telling personal stories of women who have come to the shrine seeking help and of those returning in thanksgiving. She explains that as she was going to lunch one day, she saw a young woman with her two children. The woman stopped her and told her that five years earlier she had come to Our Lady of La Leche because she was unable to have children. She prayed to Our Lady, knowing that the answer would be the will of God for her. She was back to thank Our Lady for her twins.

Those who come do not always get the answer they are hoping for, but they get an answer that brings peace, maybe not right away, but in God's time. There are as many stories as there are people who have come to kneel before Our Lady, asking her intercession.

As we leave, we feel filled with a piece of the history of our faith in America. We are nourished by the time spent with Sister and with Our Lady of La Leche. We understand a little of the peace that comes through prayer and thanksgiving. We are given a place to stay, and it is good. We are given a sense of belonging, and it is good. We are given all we need to sustain us, and as with all those who come to this "Sacred Acre," we receive the grace that is Our Lady's to give.

. . . .

Prayer

Mary, you nourish us with the gift of grace. Help us to seek what keeps us healthy in body, mind, and spirit. We understand that the more we let go and allow you into our lives, the better our lives in this world will be. Teach us to come to you and to trust and to let you lead us. In you we find safety. In you we find refuge. By you we are nourished.

. . . .

Grace

Mary provides. As she nourished Jesus, she nourishes us. She feeds us. She gives us shelter and she keeps us safe. All we have to do is trust. Even when we cannot see where she is leading, even though we do not understand at the moment, she knows. Pray to her. Trust her. Thank her.

CHAPTER FOURTEEN

. . . .

Our Lady of Prompt Succor

· ·

The French Ursuline sisters founded a convent and school for girls in New Orleans, Louisiana, in 1727. In the early 1800s when the French took possession of New Orleans, many of the sisters fled to Cuba, prompting Mother St. Andre Madier to request reinforcements from France. Her cousin, Mother St. Michel Gensoul, felt called to teach in New Orleans, but her bishop would not let her go. He told her that if the pope authorized the request, then all would be well. Pope Pius VII was virtually impossible to get in touch with because he was held captive by Napoleon and even letters were being refused. Mother petitioned the pope and prayed to Mary, promising to promote devotion to her under the title of Our Lady of

Prompt Succor if she received an answer quickly.

The pope responded immediately, the bishop honored his promise, and Mother Gensoul honored her promise to Our Lady. She commissioned a statue of Mary holding the Infant Jesus and took her to New Orleans. A few years later, a fire threatened the convent, and as everyone was being evacuated, one of the sisters took a small statue of Mary to the window and prayed to Our Lady of Prompt Succor. The wind miraculously changed the direction of the fire and the convent was saved. The small "sweetheart" statue of Mary remains in the Church of Our Lady of Prompt Succor.

During the War of 1812, New Orleans was under attack in a British effort to gain control of the Mississippi River. In 1814, Mother St. Marie Oliver deVezin ordered the statue of Our Lady of Prompt Succor to be moved to the convent chapel. The sisters, wives, and children gathered in the chapel and prayed to Our Lady for the protection of New Orleans. The British army greatly outnumbered the U.S. troops. At daybreak, Father Dubourg began Mass, and all could hear the beginnings of the war. Yet as the redcoats began to advance, a wind suddenly cleared the heavy fog that hid the men. The U.S. soldiers, down in their bunkers, easily defeated the multiple lines of marching redcoats.

In the middle of that Mass, during Communion, a courier blasted into the convent chapel to share the news of the victory. When Fr. Dubourg finished Mass, the congregation sang hymns of thanksgiving to Our Lady for the victory. Each year on January 8, Mass is sung in the Ursuline chapel in thanksgiving for the miracle. Shortly after the battle, General Andrew Jackson visited the Ursuline convent and thanked the sisters for their prayers. Our Lady of Prompt Succor is the patroness of the city of New Orleans and the state of Louisiana.

. . . .

National Shrine of Our Lady of Prompt Succor
NEW ORLEANS, LOUISIANA

Choices are made every day about where we put our time and our energy. Sometimes we choose to go out of our way for another, and usually that choice is rewarded at some point in our lives. Or, the sacrifice is just appreciated, and that is enough. When called upon by her cousin to cross the seas to a plague-ridden New Orleans and help minister and teach in the city, Mother Gensoul never could have imagined what her yes would mean to her life. She was blessed to witness more than one miracle performed after calling upon the intercession of Our Lady of Prompt Succor. The Ursuline Sisters continue to pour out the same time and energy as they teach and minister to those in New Orleans. Their daily yes in service to the needs of the community echoes that affirmative response of sisters almost two hundred years ago.

We have traveled to New Orleans to do a little work with the local Catholic bookstore. While we are there, a husband and wife, whose daughter lives in Nashville and who happen to be on the board for the Shrine of Our Lady of Prompt Succor, come into the store. This is a quick confirmation to us that we should visit the shrine. The woman spends time with us and tells us a little about the church and whom we should talk to about the shrine.

Ursuline Academy and the convent for the Ursuline Sisters share the property of the Shrine of Our Lady of Prompt Succor. When we enter the church for Mass, I can hear a couple of young people talking to a parishioner about the shrine. She is sharing the story of one of the girls from the Academy. The young girl had come to pray to Our Lady in the chapel, and while she was praying, the image of Christ appeared on one of the columns. Sister shows us a picture of the image. After all these years, Our Lady is still giving this community signs that she is with them, in good times and in bad times. Her Son is here for them just like he has always been here, especially in times when they need help quickly.

After Mass, one of the parishioners wants to make sure that we see the "sweetheart" statue in the inside chapel. The sisters were once a cloistered order, so the inside chapel is the area where they were separated from the rest of the congregation. The statue is a tiny little figure with a big history of removing obstacles in people's lives, of changing the course of damaging fire, and of bringing home safely an Air Force pilot from the war.

We go back to the sacristy to ask for more information about the shrine, and we meet one of the Sisters and the sacristan. They have been told that we may stop by after Mass. We are blessed by their help and their hospitality. Although we do not see the shadow of Christ on the column, we definitely are brought to see Christ.

. . . .

Prayer

Mary, Lady of Prompt Succor, you have offered protection in times of trouble. You know that we want to make the right choices but often take on more than we can handle, wanting to please everyone. You know we seem to always be in a hurry. Help us in our hectic lives. Help us choose where we spend our time and our energy. And when the bad part of life bears down on us, help us to see a clear path. We are thankful for your quick response to our needs. We thank you for helping us to see your Son's face.

. . . .

Grace

The city of New Orleans is filled with history and tradition and choices. As we are drawn to this particular church for Mass, we understand the significance of the vision of Christ. We understand that once again Mary is leading us to her Son. The parishioners are anxious to share the stories, just as they are to share their patroness.

CHAPTER FIFTEEN

. . . .

Our Lady of Pompeii

Bartolo Longo became a Third Order Dominican at age thirty and was known as Brother Rosary. As a lawyer, he traveled to the plain of Pompeii, Italy, to take care of the affairs of Countess De Fusco. Pompeii was filled with robbers and uneducated, poor people, suffering from a lack of faith in God. As he was walking through the church one day, he heard, "If you seek salvation, promulgate the rosary. This is Mary's one promise."

With the help of his wife, Bartolo started a confraternity of the rosary in Pompeii. He set up rosary festivals with games and races. Word got around that he needed a picture to kneel before while praying the rosary. One of the sisters at the monastery at Porta Medina had been holding on to a painting for a Dominican priest who found it at a junk dealer. Although it was in bad condition, she sent it to Bartolo. The painting portrayed Our Lady and the child Jesus handing rosaries to St. Dominic and St. Catherine, and Bartolo put the painting in a small chapel. People came to visit, and miracles occurred. Bartolo built a new church in which Mary and the child Jesus were crowned.

The painting of Our Lady was sent to Rome in 1965 and renovated. Before returning the image to Pompeii, Pope Paul VI kept it in the Vatican. He said, "Just as the image of the Virgin has been repaired and decorated, so may the image of Mary that all Christians must have within themselves be restored, renovated, and enriched" (homily, March 23, 1965).

.   .   .   .

The Shrine of Our Lady of Pompeii
CHICAGO, ILLINOIS

Still in the Easter season, the church is decorated with spring flowers and greenery. The huge wreath of flowers in the middle aisle is beautiful and makes the church feel fresh and celebratory. Behind the altar, where I would imagine the tabernacle should be, is a statue of the Risen Christ and, above, a painting of Our Lady of Pompeii. The image shows the Blessed Mother with the child Jesus on her lap. Jesus is handing the rosary to St. Dominic, while Mary hands one to St. Catherine. Our Lady has brought peace and a sense of tradition to the local Italian community since the early twentieth century, just as her rosary has brought peace to those who say the prayers and meditate on her life.

The painting of Our Lady is also high above the altar in the center of the dome. The church is dark when I make my visit, and yet I can see the beautiful artwork on the arches. In this place, there is comfort. As I pray before the tabernacle, which I find to the left of the altar, I know that many others have come here before me and found peace and a sense of belonging.

As I look up to admire the painting in the dome, I notice part of the paint peeling. My first thought is that the church is in need of repair. But, as I look around, it does not seem like it needs work. The church is quite beautiful, with high archways and rich color. The large, arched, stained-glass windows let in some light and share the artwork of the panels.

Taking time during a business trip to visit Our Lady, I know nothing about the story of Our Lady of Pompeii (who many of us might know as Our Lady of the Rosary). I get chills reading about the need for the image of Mary within ourselves to be restored, renovated, and enriched. A similar message comes from Pope Francis. We need to dig deep, to go out and repair. We must go to the recesses of the earth and teach and preach just as Dominic and Francis did. Saying we do enough in our own homes is no longer enough. There is a need to take our families with us and give them the example of service and of prayer.

The Easter season gives hope. The beauty of the season brings freshness and renews the earth. In this church, Our Lady leads us to peace and to tradition through praying the rosary, and calls us to go out and to restore.

> "One day, Brother Angelus, to your Order of Carmel the Most Blessed Virgin Mary will give a devotion to be known as the brown Scapular, and to my Order of Preachers she will give a devotion to be known as the Rosary. And, one day through the Rosary and the Scapular, Our Lady will save the world."[4]
> —St. Dominic

"She will take you into her Son's presence and use her motherly intercession with him on your behalf, so that he will be merciful toward you." [5]

—St. Catherine

. . . .

Prayer

Mary, Lady of the Rosary, as we meditate on your life, may we imitate your love. You never hesitate to reach out to the poor, to the less fortunate, and to the children. You serve all in their individual needs. Help us work to restore those who have left the Church. Teach us ways to strengthen faith in our families so that we can reach out to others. Help us to bring your children back, our families back, our world back under your loving care.

. . . .

Grace

Many times when we think we got nothing, we may just have it all. When we let things settle, answers come. When we rest, our vision is clear. When we pray, good things happen.

CHAPTER SIXTEEN

. . . .

Our Lady of Banneux

I have come to relieve the suffering." In 1933 in Banneux, Belgium, Mariette Beco saw Our Lady from her kitchen window outside in the garden. Her mother did not let her go outside because it was too late and cold. Several days later, Mariette went to the garden, and as she prayed the rosary, Our Lady appeared and prayed with her.

Eight times she appeared, dressed in white with a blue sash and a transparent veil covering her head, with a golden rose on her foot and a rosary over her arm. She showed Mariette a stream, "for all the nations...to bring comfort to the sick." She told her that she is the "Virgin of the Poor," and she asked her to "pray hard." Mariette did everything Our Lady asked of her. She even asked for a sign for the local priest, but Our Lady responded, "Believe in me. I will believe in you."

The Beco family returned to church and prayed the rosary daily. Despite ridicule from their friends and neighbors, they continued to believe and to trust in the visions of Our Lady. During the fourth apparition, Mariette asked Our Lady what she could do for her, and Mary replied, "I would like a small chapel." A chapel was built where Mary requested it, and many have been cured at the spring. In 2008, Mariette made a final statement, "I was no more than a postman who delivers the mail. Once this has been done, the postman is of no importance anymore."

.   .   .   .

Virgin of the Poor Shrine
New Hope, Tennessee

The signs are made of wood, with the letters burned in: S-H-R-I-N-E. The wood forms an arrow, which points us down winding roads to the next sign. There comes a point when we are riding on a one-lane street. Together we go in, and together we come out.

Incredibly deep in the woods off Interstate 24, the Catholic Church owns six hundred acres, donated by the Duncan family. The Benedictine Monks and local craftsmen built the Virgin of the Poor Shrine under the direction of Father Basil Mattingly, O.S.B. The setting is similar to the location of the shrine in Belgium. Above the stone archway of the small chapel is a mosaic of Our Lady appearing to Mariette. The young girl kneels in prayer with Our Lady. This place, too, is a place of prayer. Inside there is a simple stone altar and a mosaic of the Crucifixion with St. John and Our Lady: "Behold, your Mother."

Cars begin pulling up to the shrine, one behind the other, and people join one another at the tables near the parking lot. They are plugging in Crock-Pots and spreading tablecloths, gathering as they do every Sunday from May to October to share a meal and to pray the Stations together. We are invited, and although we cannot stay, we know we are always welcome. We have come to this small place to visit Our Lady, and we find a group of people who gather to pray because they believe.

God's signs are all over the world. We are asked to follow, to believe, to go, to join one another in prayer. We find Christ in one another, in the breaking of the bread.

. . . .

Prayer

Mary, you come to us in our poverty, and all you ask is for us to believe, for us to pray, for us to follow. In our spiritual needs, in our physical needs, in our mental needs, strengthen us. Give us the courage to recognize our own failings, to pray, and to allow your intercession for comfort and healing.

. . . .

Grace

We are tentative about the drive down the winding, slim streets to this shrine of Our Lady. For some reason, we never feel like we are headed in the right direction, despite the signs. As people begin driving into the parking lot, we feel the need to leave, but they know no strangers. They welcome us. This shrine, Our Lady, is for all. There is a feeling of belonging to something bigger, something familiar. We are included, despite our poverties, despite our weaknesses. We feel comfort.

CHAPTER SEVENTEEN

. . . .

Consecration to Jesus through Mary

. . . .

Maximilian Kolbe was a young child when Our Lady appeared to him. He asked her about his future, and she held out two crowns, one white and one red. She asked him which crown he would choose for his life, the white for a life of purity or the red to be a martyr. Maximilian said, "I choose both."

Maximilian entered the Conventual Franciscan Order in 1910, and after spending time in Rome, returned to Poland and founded the Militia of the Immaculate, a movement of Marian consecration. He in turn founded the City of the Immaculate, which expanded to house nearly nine hundred friars. They published devotional information, a daily newspaper, and a monthly magazine. They even started their own radio show. In 1930, he founded the City of the Immaculate in Japan. His goal was to lead individuals with Mary to Jesus. "My aim is to institute perpetual adoration, the most important activity."

Nazis imprisoned Maximilian in 1941. After the escape of a few of the prisoners, ten men were chosen to die in the starvation bunker. One of the men chosen called out, asking what would happen to his wife and child. Maximilian offered to take his place in the bunker. Every day, he prayed the Mass and sang songs to Mary along with the other men. When the guards came to check after two weeks, Maximilian was the only prisoner still alive. The impatient guards finally gave him a lethal injection.

. . . .

Marytown, National Shrine of St. Maximilian Kolbe
LIBERTYVILLE, ILLINOIS

Marytown, a Conventual Franciscan friary, is a place of spiritual renewal, a place of prayer, and a place where we can make an act of consecration to Mary Immaculate. The work of Maximilian Kolbe, to spread devotion to Our Lady and through her lead us to Jesus, continues today in Marytown. My daughter and I realize that this place may not necessarily be a specific shrine to Our Lady, but with the name "Marytown," we have to visit. We do not know much about Maximilian Kolbe when we arrive, but we sure know the story of his life when we leave.

Of course the first place we approach is Our Lady of the Blessed Sacrament Perpetual Adoration Chapel, patterned after St. Paul Outside-the-Walls in Rome. With the mosaics and the stained glass of Mary and Maximilian Kolbe, our eyes are all over the chapel, but the ultimate draw is straight down to the large monstrance behind the altar. Under a large dome, guarded by angels, Jesus awaits us in the monstrance. It is for him that Mary has brought us to her place. It is for him that we kneel in adoration. It is for him that others are kneeling all around us.

The pure white statue of Our Lady of the Blessed Sacrament is also in front. She stands with her Son, holding the chalice and the Host, offering them to us. They are immaculate—stark white. They wait for all to come. We visit the side chapel of the Sorrowful Mother, which displays images of the seven sorrows of Mary on the walls and shares with us Mary's suffering with her Son. There is a Kolbe chapel, with a first-classic relic. It is below a mosaic rich in color that tells the story of Mary's love for this saint and his complete gift of himself to others and to Christ. I pray he brings more people to this place of consecration.

We continue to the conference center, visiting the Holocaust exhibit and the beautiful gift shop. We learn a lot about the life and death and work of St. Maximilian. And we learn about consecration to Mary.

The outside areas are certainly worth a little of our time also. The Rosary Garden is our favorite, with the large, stark-white shrines of each of the mysteries, the beautiful gardens that surround each area, and the benches offering places to rest. It reflects Mary's goodness and grace. There is a shrine to Our Lady of Lourdes and Our Lady of Fatima as well as to the Sacred Heart of Jesus, the crucifixion, and the Infant of Prague.

Enrollment in the Militia of the Immaculata is recommended on a Marian Feast Day: January 1 (Solemnity of Mary), February 11 (Our Lady of Lourdes), March 25 (Annunciation), May 13 (Our Lady of Fatima), May 31 (Visitation), June 27 (Our Lady of Perpetual Help), July 16 (Our Lady of Mt. Carmel), August 15 (Assumption), August 22 (Queenship of Mary), September 8 (Birth of the Blessed Virgin Mary), September 15 (Our Lady of Sorrows), October 7 (Our Lady of the Rosary), November 21 (Presentation of Mary), December 8 (Immaculate Conception), or December 12 (Our Lady of Guadalupe).

> "My hope for you is that with every passing day and every passing moment you will get closer to Mary Immaculate. May you come to know her ever better and love her ever more." [6]
>
> —St. Maximilian Kolbe

. . . .

Prayer

Mary Immaculate, Lady of the Blessed Sacrament, strengthen our love for you by helping us to set aside ourselves to better serve your Son. Help us as we strive to frequent the sacrament of reconciliation, attend Mass, and pray the rosary each day. Through your purity, may we be made pure. As you offer your Son in the Eucharist, may we accept him into our hearts. Help us find time to visit your Son in the Blessed Sacrament that we may draw ever closer to him. Mary, intercede for us to your Son.

. . . .

Grace

Moments of grace are often found in the most unexpected places. Often, when we just happen off the street to visit, that is when we gain the greatest rewards. Mary invites us to consecrate ourselves to her, one-on-one. Together, we are blessed.

CHAPTER EIGHTEEN

. . . .

Our Lady of Schoenstatt

In 1914 in Vallendar, Germany, Father Joseph Kentenich decided to turn the St. Michael Chapel at Schoenstatt into a place for Mary. He was prompted by a newspaper article about the place of pilgrimage, Valle di Pompeii in Italy, started by Bartolo Longo, a convert from atheism (see chapter fifteen). He wanted a place where Mary could distribute grace. He and his students worked by the motto, "Nothing without you—nothing without us." They brought to the shrine their everyday lives and experiences, and they offered them to Mary to work her miracles of grace. They viewed all happenings as Divine Providence.

Today there are more than two hundred shrines spread all over the world. The Schoenstatt shrines and spiritual centers offer families and individuals spiritual nourishment, renewal, and continuing support through retreats, camps, and monthly group meetings. Pilgrims find that as they offer themselves to Our Lady, they receive the grace they need to live the Gospel.

. . . .

Schoenstatt Shrine
WAUKESHA, WISCONSIN

Many events happen in our lives that make a huge impact, while we may just call them coincidence. Then, we look back at the day and we realize and recognize God's hand in the moment, Divine Providence.

My daughter and I drive slowly down the driveway, wondering where exactly Our Lady has led us in this place called Waukesha. Near the end of the property, we find a small, steep-roofed chapel beside which two sisters are planting flowers. Another sister is driving around in a golf cart with a family in tow. We slowly approach, not knowing what to expect, and ask if we can enter the chapel. "Oh yes. Please." The response is short and to the point. I like it. We enter and find kneelers, a small altar with a tabernacle, a picture of Mary, a crucifix, and candles. We take time in front of the tabernacle with a picture above of Our Lady holding her Son. The words wrapped around the frame, *"Servus Mariae Nunquam Peribit,"* translate to "A child (a servant) of Mary will never perish." She is our protection, and kneeling before her, we feel the warmth of her as a mother.

As we leave the chapel, we wander down through the property to the Stations of the Cross and the cemetery. The land and the landscape are beautiful. Every plant and every rock are in place. We walk back up to the chapel and enter for a few more minutes, then take a few moments to talk to the gardeners. They are passionate about their work and the shrine. They suggest we go to the retreat house and talk to the Sister there, "She will tell you the story." What they could have said is, "She will share her gift of faith. She will teach you and she will share the grace that comes from taking the time to visit Our Lady."

The sister at the door to the retreat house tells us that Sister Maria is busy but invites us in after hearing of our project and tells us the entire story of Schoenstatt. She generously offers us the gift of her time. She tells us the story of a young girl entering the chapel and immediately recognizing it as the chapel of her hometown. Sister says that one of the special gifts is that every chapel is identical inside, having been built based on the original shrine, giving the visitor the feeling of being at home, being in a familiar place. This is the same thing I love about the Catholic Church. No matter where we travel, we hear the same words and share in the same Body of Christ. Sister cannot be nicer, and she helps us to start our trek of shrines through Wisconsin on the right foot. She says it's Divine Providence that we are here, and the gardeners said the same. We have no doubt.

. . . .

Prayer

Mary, source of grace, help us to rest in the holy places you have had your hand in providing for us here. Help us to be at home where we find your Son. As we bring our everyday lives to you, work your miracles for us. We offer you all we are, all we do, and all we have. Give us the grace to do the will of the Father. Help us to trust in Divine Providence.

. . . .

Grace

In God's house, all is the same. We are at home. We are comfortable. We may bring our entire lives to him, and he will love us unconditionally. He will never change. As we follow his will, he will work miracles.

CHAPTER NINETEEN

. . . .

Mary, Help of Christians

. . . .

In the sixteenth century, the title Mary, Help of Christians, was given to the Blessed Mother after the Battle of Lepanto when Christian naval forces defeated the Ottoman fleet.

The Feast of Mary, Help of Christians, was instituted by Pope Pius VII in the nineteenth century. The pope was imprisoned by Napoleon for nine years, and after the Battle of Leipzig, on the Feast of Our Lady of Mercy, he was released in Savona. On his journey back to Rome, he visited many sanctuaries of Mary and crowned her images. He finally made it to Rome on May 24, only to have to return to Savona. After the Congress of Vienna and the battle of Waterloo, Pope Pius VII again returned to Rome and declared May 24 the Feast of Mary, Help of Christians, in thanksgiving for his safety.

St. John Bosco had a great devotion to Mary, Help of Christians, and built a basilica in her honor in Turin. He founded the Salesian Congregation and a religious congregation for women and dedicated both to Mary under the title Help of Christians.

. . . .

Basilica of the National Shrine of Mary, Help of Christians
HUBERTUS, WISCONSIN

As we approach the Basilica of the National Shrine of Mary, understandably referred to as Holy Hill, darkness has set in on our morning, and the steeples are peeking out from the trees as in some mysterious castle setting from long ago. As we get closer, we expect the drawbridge to lower and allow us to enter. I have to stop at the bottom and take pictures, holding up a few cars.

We stop first at the Our Lady of Lourdes Shrine and spend some time in thanksgiving for safety. I dip my hands into the water and rub it on my foot, which seems to have an occasional strange cramp. We look down through the woods and see the Stations of the Cross winding down the hill, though the impending rain will keep us from praying the Stations the way they are intended for pilgrims.

As we climb the stairs to the main church, we can only imagine what it was like before they put in the elevator and would carry those who could not walk up the stairs. The observation platforms were closed due to the high winds. At the entrance, Mary, Help of Christians, stands as patroness. We enter and spend most of our time in awe of the stained-glass windows. Many of the windows tell the life of Our Lady, and several tell of the Carmelite Order, especially of Mary giving the brown Scapular to St. Simon Stock.

Above the tabernacle behind the altar is an arched mosaic of the Trinity, with Mary and Joseph and the twelve apostles. The two side altars have mosaics of St. Teresa of Avila and St. John of the Cross. The basilica and national shrine are run by the Discalced Carmelites. As we enter the Shrine Chapel, we see the breathtaking image of Mary standing with the child Jesus. They are dressed in gold, and Jesus's heart is exposed, and his hand is raised in blessing. At their feet are bronze roses. She is Our Lady of Holy Hill. Outside her chapel are racks of crutches left by pilgrims who have received favors from Our Lady's intercession to our merciful Father.

There is so much more to this place; the St. Thérèse chapel, the monastery, and the guest house. We read in some of the small areas about the Carmelites. We see the fifteen-foot cross that was carried to the top of the hill and placed on the summit by town residents. We read about the first two shrines and the purchase of the property in 1855 for fifty dollars. We are amazed at the stories, the beauty, and the simplicity. The presence of the Discalced Carmelites brings a peaceful, simple, prayerful atmosphere, just as prescribed by St. Teresa of Avila for the renewal of the Church. Here, we find a place to rest our souls.

. . . .

Prayer

Mary, Help of Christians, be with us in our everyday battles. Save us from this world of violence and anger. Teach us to simplify. Teach us to carry the banner of love and bring the world back under your protection and care. Give us peace. Help us to find rest.

. . . .

Grace

In this world where more is better, we learn in this place that the less we have, the less we have to fight about. We learn the need to live simply. Our lives can still be filled with beauty and be simple.

. . . .

CHAPTER TWENTY

NEVER FORGET

Our Lady of Good Help

. . . .

"I am the Queen of Heaven who prays for the conversion of sinners, and I wish you to do the same. Gather the children in this wild country and teach them what they should know for salvation."[7]

In 1859, Adele Brise left Belgium with her family and settled near Green Bay, Wisconsin. Four years later, as she was walking to the gristmill, she saw a lady dressed all in white standing between two trees. She froze, not really knowing what to say or do until the vision disappeared.

The following Sunday, walking to Mass with her sister Isabel and a friend, Adele again saw the lady in white between the same two trees. After Mass, she told her confessor about the appearance, and he suggested she ask the lady her name and what she wants. Adele approached the lady, who was clothed in white with a yellow sash around her waist and a crown of stars on her head. "In God's name, who are you and what do you want of me?" Our Lady revealed herself as the Queen of Heaven and asked Adele to teach the children in the area the catechism, how to make the sign of the cross, and how to receive the sacraments.

Adele started immediately teaching children the catechism and pointing out to adults their sins against God. She went from house to house with the work of Our Lady's request. Finally some other women joined her, and they were able to open St. Mary's Boarding Academy, so the children could come to them. Her father built the first chapel between the trees, and many from the Belgian community helped to build the school and a convent.

People began coming to the chapel, and miracles and healings occurred. In 1871 as the Great Peshtigo Fire took the lives of more than fifteen hundred people in the Green Bay area, many came to the chapel for refuge. Adele and the sisters took the statue of Our Lady outside and processed around the property with all the people. The fire reached the fence, but spread no farther. Each year, on August 15, the Feast of the Assumption, the bishop and crowds of people gather in procession to pray the rosary and celebrate Mass.

. . . .

Shrine of Our Lady of Good Help
New Franken, Wisconsin

"Go and fear nothing. I will help you."[8] Our Lady's words to Adele are timeless.

As my daughter and I drive up to the church, there are pilgrims just like us wandering around. We wonder why we have not heard more about this approved apparition site right here in our own country. The bishop approved it in 2010, and I must not have been listening. Or, I didn't want to. A customer had come into our store one day, and when he heard about our visiting shrines, he left this information on a card for me, telling me, "You need to visit this place."

We go directly to the church to visit Our Lord and to be grateful for the journey. Behind the altar, the words "Ave Maria" stretch out above a beautiful image of Mary presenting her Son. The statue stands above the tabernacle, which is flanked by two angels kneeling in adoration. To the right of the altar is an image of Mary as described by Adele during the apparitions, dressed in white with a yellow sash and crown of stars around her head. She brings us to pause and reflect.

We go down below the church to the crypt and find a statue of Our Lady with outstretched arms over the place where the apparitions occurred. One of the Fathers of Mercy, directors of the shrine, is bowed in prayer. There is no doubt that we stand on holy ground.

As we walk the outside Stations of the Cross and rosary walk, we follow a family of girls with their mother. Despite the rough ground, the sisters push their mom around the yard in her wheelchair. Just as Adele trudged from house to house in all kinds of weather teaching the children, these girls struggle, but keep right on plodding from prayer to prayer. There is talk of quitting, but we watch them to the end. This shrine stands as a place where all have persevered, despite the difficulties to do all that is asked, with Our Lady's help.

. . . .

Prayer

Our Lady of Good Help, you came to the aid of Adele many times as she persevered doing the work you asked her to do. Help us first to listen and to follow our calling. Then, we beg you, help us to persevere.

. . . .

Grace

We stand on holy ground and witness the prayerful perseverance of a group of women. As one wants to stop, the other energizes the group. Despite our struggles, faith will see us through to the end. Fear nothing.

. . . .

CHAPTER TWENTY-ONE

Our Lady of Guadalupe

. . . .

"I wish and intensely desire that in this place my sanctuary be erected so that in it I may show and make known and give all my love, my compassion, my help and my protection to the people. I am your merciful Mother."[9]

On December 9, 1531, Juan Diego, a Mexican peasant and a convert to the Catholic faith, was on his way to Mass in honor of the Blessed Mother. When he reached the base of Tepeyac Hill, he heard what he thought were birds singing. Then, he heard a voice call his name, so he climbed the hill. When he reached the top, he found a young woman surrounded by light who spoke to him in his native language, Nahuatl. She asked him to have a church built there in her honor.

Juan Diego went to the bishop and waited a long time to see him and tell him what the woman had requested. Juan returned and told Mary that he felt the bishop did not believe him. She asked him to go again. Juan Diego waited again, and this time the bishop asked him many questions and told him to bring back a sign that the woman was truly the Blessed Mother. The Blessed Mother asked him to return the next day, when she would have a sign for the bishop.

But Juan Diego's uncle was sick, and he did not go to the hill. When his uncle requested last rites, Juan Diego hurried to get a priest. He tried to avoid Our Lady, worried about his sick uncle, but Mary came to him and told him not to worry about his uncle because she would see that he would be cured. She asked Juan Diego to climb the hill and cut the Castilian roses he would find blooming there, although it was the dead of winter. She arranged them in his tilma and sent him once again to the bishop with her message. Again, Juan Diego was made to wait a long time. When he entered the office, he knelt before the bishop and opened his tilma, dropping roses to the floor. But the bishop then saw an image of Our Lady on the tilma and fell to his knees. The following day, Juan Diego showed the bishop the place where he should build the church. The Basilica of Our Lady of Guadalupe in Mexico is today one of the most visited Marian shrines in the world. Pope John Paul II named Our Lady of Guadalupe patroness of the Americas in 1999.

. . . .

Shrine of Our Lady of Guadalupe
La Crosse, Wisconsin

God often chooses the ones we would least expect, the meek and the mild, the weak and the lowly. He knows they are prepared to accept the responsibility that comes from having been chosen. In their humility, in their silence, they speak volumes.

The volunteers and workers at the Shrine of Our Lady are special. As with many shrines we visit, they each come with a different gift necessary to make the visit memorable. As we enter, the man at the information desk is incredibly enthusiastic. He cannot wait for us to experience the shrine. He seems genuinely enamored by the journey we are about to take and points out little tidbits we may miss if we are on our own self-guided tour.

We begin our ascent with apprehension, much like Juan Diego as he responded to Our Lady's voice, wondering what we could possibly find on this long, uphill climb. Despite it being the month of June, we are chilled in the early morning air. The first stop, the Votive Candle Chapel, warms us with the burning lights of love for Our Lady. The colorful stained-glass windows of Our Lady of Knock, Our Lady of Loreto, Our Lady of the Miraculous Medal, Mother of Good Counsel, Our Lady of Fatima, Our Lady of Sorrows, and Our Lady of Lourdes make us pause in prayer and thanksgiving. Considering the journey we have undertaken visiting Marian shrines, this small chapel is packed full of confirmation.

The trek up the hill includes stops along the way for reflection and rest. A bronze figure of St. Kateri Tekakwitha is filled with details of this young girl's love for Christ. The braid, the feather, and the fringe around her top and skirt identify her as our Native American saint. The rosary wrapped through her fingers and her fixed gaze upon the cross cradled in her arm testify to her faith and gratitude to Christ crucified. She certainly was one who suffered ridicule and torture for what she holds before us.

The next resting place is marked with a bronze sculpture of the Holy Family. The man from the information desk gave us the clue that Mary's expression says it all. He is spot on. As Joseph teaches Jesus the family trade, Mary looks on, somewhat shocked that the two pieces of wood they hold while working together form a cross. The family's entire life was a preparation of what was to come, a journey to the cross. In the background, Bishop Raymond Burke, the founder of the shrine, stands with the donors of the initial property for the shrine.

As we reached the basilica, we look for a moment at the large bronze statue of Juan Diego opening his tilma for the bishop, who discovers not only the Castilian roses but also the image of Our Lady. The basilica is a gallery of those who gave their lives to Christ, who are examples to us of how to live and how to love. Huge paintings of St. Thérèse of Lisieux, Blessed Miguel Pro, St. Gianna Beretta Molla, St. Peregrine, St. Maria Goretti, and St. Faustina Kowalska line the side aisles of the church. Behind the altar, the mosaic of Our Lady of Guadalupe above the tabernacle gives honor to our Mother of the Americas. The ceiling of the narthex is filled with a mural of the apparitions at Tepeyac Hill, and more images of saints are in the lower narthex.

As we leave, the morning has passed and the warm sun is bursting through the trees. Visiting the Memorial for the Unborn, we notice the light leading us directly to Our Lady holding three tiny infants. We walk the Stations of the Cross up to the beautiful Rosary Walk, with panels of hand-painted blue tiles depicting the individual mysteries. We are tired. We know now why so many we pass on the way back down the hill to the Pilgrim Center are in golf carts.

Yet we talk the entire way back about the incredible layout and planning of this place built for us. This shrine where we spend half our day, and could easily spend the other half, is built just as the one on Tepeyac Hill, so that we can have a place where Mary, Our Mother, can come and give us her love, her compassion, her help, and her protection. And we are filled to the brim with not just the gifts from Our Lady, but also from those who are there and those who have come to visit alongside us.

. . . .

The Shrine of Our Lady of Guadalupe
SANTE FE, NEW MEXICO

The statue of Our Lady of Guadalupe outside the small adobe church stands near the road for all to see and take notice. Its base is filled with flowers of devotion. The rosary circles the statue, and each large round marking on the sidewalk contains the words of the Hail Mary, as we walk the mysteries directly up to the crucifix. She is constantly leading us to her Son. As we leave, there are several people praying at the statue. She is right there, for the convenience of the city.

The oldest church in the United States dedicated to Our Lady of Guadalupe, this is believed to have been built as a shrine around 1777. We have to step up and duck our heads to get in the front door. We are immediately drawn to the front of the church. Our Lady is on a large panel, with the story of Juan Diego around her. To the right of the altar is a heart-shaped votive candle holder near a large image of Our Lady. My youngest child lights a candle and then files into the pew to pray. On the left side of the altar, Juan Diego kneels in prayer. The shrine is peaceful. We are alone for the moment, except for Our Lady.

. . . .

Prayer

Our Lady of Guadalupe—Patroness of the Americas—often you reveal your great love for us through the people we least expect, through a short encounter or through a simple meeting. Help us to wait patiently, to listen, to be attentive to those you put in our path. May we hear your voice and may we respond to your requests, as you did, with a simple yes.

. . . .

Grace

There are many who have taken the time to listen and to answer the call to lead others to Christ, and all we have to do is find a small bit of humility to allow the least expected and the smallest to teach us. We tend to think we know it all, have seen it all, and do not need help from others. But when we allow ourselves, when we humble ourselves, we receive the true gifts that await us.

. . . .

CHAPTER TWENTY-TWO

Our Lady of San Juan de Los Lagos

. . . .

A small statue of the Immaculate Conception was brought to the village of San Juan, Mexico, by Spanish missionaries. The statue was placed in the church to promote devotion to Our Lady.

A group of acrobats that were performing in small towns as they traveled through Mexico in 1623 stopped in San Juan de Los Lagos. To heighten excitement, swords were placed on the ground beneath their act. During the routine, their young daughter slipped and, landing on the swords, was killed. The parents, overwhelmed with sadness, wrapped her body and took her to the Chapel of Our Lady. The caretaker of the chapel asked the family to put their trust in Our Lady and, taking the statue from the altar, put it on the dead girl's body. Suddenly, the girl came back to life. Pilgrims began to visit the chapel as word of the miracle spread and devotion grew to Our Lady under the title Our Lady of San Juan de Los Lagos.

Seeing that the statue was made of cornstalks and glue and in sad condition, the acrobat asked the pastor of the chapel if he could take the statue to a local artist for repair. The pastor allowed him to take the statue, and the artist repaired the image of Our Lady to perfect condition, actually more beautiful than before. When the man went to pay him, the artist could not be found. The statue was placed back in the chapel, and pilgrims began coming from all over, seeking miracles, praying for cures, and bringing gifts to place before Our Lady. A larger church was built to accommodate the thousands of pilgrims who come to pray with Our Lady today.

. . . .

Basilica of Our Lady of San Juan del Valle National Shrine

SAN JUAN, TEXAS

The four-hour drive through cattle ranches and cacti from San Antonio to San Juan is tedious but all a part of the journey. As we arrive at the shrine and check into our room, we decide to go straight to Saturday night Mass. This basilica was built after a low-flying plane crashed into St. John the Baptist Church, destroying the shrine but sparing the fifty priests concelebrating Mass and the fifty people in attendance. As the plane burst into flames, a couple of the priests and the sacristan saved the statue of Our Lady of San Juan and the Blessed Sacrament.

Everything about the basilica is moving. A mariachi band that plays for Mass is completely dressed in green and wearing gold neck scarves with, I believe, the image of Our Lady. The priest begins Mass by asking for full participation from adults as well as children. He asks families to help their children stand and kneel at the appropriate times. It is a good reminder for us all. Pay attention. Be ready. Christ will show up. We are moved by the enthusiasm of the priest and the band. We are moved by the participation of the families and by the full flowing responses of the people. Father's homily is about resting in the arms of Jesus. We are reminded to rest. Traveling can be intense: arriving where you need to be when you need to be, scheduling, flying, renting, driving, arriving, and departing just to do it all over again. We are prompted to rest.

He goes on to talk about hope and tradition and family. He speaks of the profound faith of the people who come to the shrine. He comments on the generosity of the many humble Mexican-American farmworkers who sacrifice to build up and to maintain this house of prayer. He stresses the importance of passing the traditions of faith on to our young people, just as parents passed on the desire to visit Our Lady at the shrine. His passion for all that the shrine stands for comes through, and I am wondering if the people around me might burst out in agreement. All are silent. All are deep in prayer.

During the consecration, as Father holds the Body of Christ up to the congregation, everyone responds, "My Lord and My God," together in a shout of belief. A response that usually resonates only within my heart echoes instead throughout the entire church. And again, the priest holds up the Precious Blood and all respond, "My Lord and My God." The people here want to shout it to the rooftops. The reverence, the celebration, the participation, the prayer at the end before Our Lady, brings a simple, weary traveler to rest in our Father's arms.

Sunday we go to breakfast in the cafeteria and meet a woman, a homegrown, whose parents made the pilgrimage to the shrine on foot fifteen miles each way when she was young. She explains the impact those journeys made on her life: "Now that's a strong devotion." And that's exactly what I think this encounter has proved to be—a great sense of devotion to Our Lady, a constant, continual flow of devotion, love and faith. The homegrown is here now, maybe by bus, but she is here.

We spend the day walking the bigger-than-life-sized Stations of the Cross and then go back into the shrine and visit behind the altar in the vision room and the Milagros area. Along with family pictures, holy cards, and private notes, milagros (small charms made of different materials), are attached to the large cross in the center of the room and around the different devotion areas such as St. Charbel, Our Lady of Schoenstatt, and Divine Niño. These charms signify the needs of the pilgrims—the requests for intercession and for healing. There are flowers and candles everywhere. The people who have come to visit have come with their traditions and with their families. We pray with them. We light the candles for our family, and we read the stories. Through it all, we hear the resounding response, "My Lord and My God."

The kneelers are constantly emptied and refilled with the flow of pilgrims. There is a Mass every two hours from seven to seven. The mariachi band plays at every Mass. We see Sister Rose, whom we had met selling dinners the night before, and during lunch she tells us all about the original church. She meets us later and drives us over, giving us a bag of brochures and other information. She tells us about the history and the love of the poor people to give the work of their hands to rebuild and to maintain this place for Mary. They are hardworking, and they come here with their families, as we are learning, to rest in the arms of Jesus.

. . . .

Prayer

Virgin of San Juan, you bring together our families in faith and tradition. Help us to know the importance of passing this on to our children. Help us not to be afraid to live in the truth. As we celebrate the same Mass all over the world, may we proclaim with confidence, "My Lord and My God!"

. . . .

Grace

We have come to a church that is full at every Mass. The same band finds it a privilege to play for every Mass. We are asked to participate fully in the real presence of Christ. We are with large, extended families who share the richness of the Spirit. We are truly moved beyond words.

CHAPTER TWENTY-THREE

. . . .

Our Lady of Martyrs

The Shrine of Our Lady of Martyrs in Auriesville, New York, is believed to be the area of the seventeenth-century Mohawk village of Ossernenon. On this land, three Jesuit missionaries were martyred, and our first Native American saint was born.

In 1642, Father Isaac Jogues and Brother Rene Goupil were brought to Ossernenon from the Jesuit missions of Canada as captives. They had come from France to spread the faith to the Indians. On the way back from praying the rosary together, the Jesuits saw two Indians waiting for them. They knew there was possible trouble. As they crossed the bridge, one of the Indians pulled out a tomahawk and killed Br. Rene

Goupil, whose last word was, "Jesus." Fr. Isaac Jogues knelt to receive his strike, but he was left unharmed, so he anointed his Jesuit Brother.

Fr. Isaac learned later that Goupil was martyred because he was seen the day before blessing a little boy with the sign of the cross. Fr. Isaac Jogues escaped to France but later returned accompanied by John de Lalande, a teenager working with the Jesuit missions in Canada for peace negotiations, bringing with him a black box filled with items he needed to say Mass. Suddenly, Indians were dying of an epidemic and crops were going bad, and the people blamed the black box, calling it a demon. Fr. Isaac was killed upon his return to the village, and the next day, his companion, John de Lalande, was killed.

Ten years after the deaths of the three martyrs, Kateri Tekakwitha was born to a Mohawk chief and an Algonquin captive at the village of Ossernenon. When her parents and brother died of smallpox, Kateri went to live with her uncle. Her mother had been Catholic, and Kateri longed to be baptized. One day in 1675, when Kateri was home with a hurt foot, a so-called Black Robe (Jesuit priest), Fr. James de Lamberville, came to the door, and Kateri expressed her baptism wish. Father explained the problems she would face trying to live as a Christian in her village but Kateri was persistent in her plea. On Easter Sunday, April 5, 1676, Kateri was baptized.

Her family, however, did not understand this devotion to the Catholic faith. Kateri's uncle ridiculed and picked on her and left her without food, but despite the hardship, she went to Mass twice a day. She eventually escaped to Canada and lived with other converts. She learned more about the faith, prayed the rosary, and made her first Communion. She made a private vow to God and had a reputation of holiness. Sick most of her life, Kateri's declining health caused her to have to stay in bed for days at a time. She suffered terribly from high fevers and pain throughout her entire body. She remained devoted to prayer and sacrifice up until her last day. Kateri was only twenty-four years old when she died.

Sacrificing their lives to spread the Catholic faith, the three Jesuit missionaries along with Kateri Tekakwitha are recognized as martyrs of the Church. Our Lady understands what it is to give your very life for the love of the people, for the Church. When Fr. Joseph Loyzance purchased this property in 1884, he named it "Our Lady of Martyrs" after the Blessed Mother who suffered at the foot of the cross of her Son.

. . . .

National Shrine of the North American Martyrs
AURIESVILLE, NEW YORK

A beautiful drive along the Hudson River brings us to a good-sized piece of land filled with crosses, signs, and statues. We are a little reluctant to learn of the extreme suffering that has happened where we stand, yet we keep in mind the reality of how many conversions have taken place on this land. We read and learn about the amazing Jesuits that came from France to bring the Native Americans to Christ. The hard work of these men and the example of their faith and courage is what moves us.

We enter the Coliseum of Our Lady of Martyrs and are overwhelmed with all there is to see. The many-sided altar area with the shrines of the martyrs and Our Lady are made of pointed tipped logs lined next to one another. The logs, like the trees outside, are marked with a red cross and often with the name of Jesus. Fr. Isaac marked the trees in this way to keep the name of Jesus in front of them at all times. The statue of Kateri is adorned with several rosaries around her neck. The church is built in the round, with a three-tiered ceiling signifying the Trinity. There are seventy-two doors for the seventy-two disciples, and above the eight double doors are the statues of the North American martyrs. The twelve tiers of pews symbolize the apostles.

Outside, we take our time walking around the front and seeing the beautiful Fatima statue and the view across the valley. There is an area, Theresa's Rosary, with the rosary made out of stones in the ground. A thirteen-year-old Huron girl, brought as a captive with Fr. Isaac, would say the rosary in secret from the Indians who had taken her rosary away. There is an area with crosses with the images of the seven sorrows of Mary and large colored images of the Stations of the Cross. The Ravine is the area where Br. Rene was martyred. The *Pietá* statue is the original statue from the first chapel, and there is a beautiful Wayside Shrine of the Madonna and Child and a Lourdes Grotto.

The land is filled with shrines to Our Lady. We feel that she holds the first martyr of the Church in her arms. She is here to console, love, and witness to the pain and the suffering. In her loving arms we are consoled. We also understand that the rosary is a great devotion during the times of struggle and of fear. There is power in the rosary, in the seven sorrows of Mary, and in the Mass. This shrine is the example of the strength we gain to defend our faith when Our Lady is by our side. This shrine is a beautiful witness to the work of conversion.

. . . .

Prayer

Mary, bless us with the example of our martyrs. These men were faithful to God and to you. These men took the chance and lost their lives spreading the Gospel. These men were hated and yet they loved. They were tortured and yet they loved. They feared and yet they loved.

Teach us to have the strength and the will to do the work of conversion in your name. Help us to form habits of praying the rosary and going to Mass. Teach us your ways, that we may always defend the faith.

. . . .

Grace

In this place, we receive the grace to fully experience the history of our saints and martyrs. These people suffered horribly. We are moved by what they have done in the name of the Catholic faith. And, the example of the young Kateri—not worrying about what others think or say—fills us with humility. She understood at a young age what it meant to truly follow Jesus. We are better for visiting, and we are blessed by a Mother who holds us, even in our deepest sorrow.

. . . .

CHAPTER TWENTY-FOUR

Our Lady of Fatima

"In the end, my Immaculate Heart will triumph; the Holy Father will consecrate Russia to me, she will be converted, and a period of peace will be granted to the world."[10]

In 1917, the Blessed Mother appeared to three shepherd children, Lucia, Jacinta, and Francisco, in the village of Fatima in Portugal. She appeared to them five more times, and on July 13 gave them messages to be spread throughout the world. The messages, known as the Three Secrets of Fatima, consisted of a vision of hell along with instructions on how to save sinners and establish devotion to her Immaculate

Heart. She told of the consecration of Russia to her Immaculate Heart and warned of famines and wars and deaths if the world did not stop offending God.

She asked the children to spread the importance of the Communion of Reparation on the First Saturdays. Mary promised to "assist at the moment of death, with all graces necessary for salvation, all those who, on the first Saturday of five consecutive months shall confess, receive holy Communion, recite five decades of the Rosary, and keep Me company for fifteen minutes while meditating on the fifteen mysteries of the Rosary, with the intention of making reparation to Me." She also requested the prayer after each decade of the rosary: "Oh my Jesus, forgive us our sins, save us from the fires of hell. Lead all souls to heaven, especially those most in need of your mercy."[11]

The three children were interrogated for several days by the district administrator, Artur de Oliveira Santos. They were kidnapped August 13 and put in jail, where their captors threatened to boil them in hot oil. Even though they were separated from one another, their stories remained the same, and they never gave in to letting out the secret Our Lady had asked them to keep. The children were finally returned to Fatima, where the apparitions continued.

On October 13, during her last apparition, as Mary promised, she sent a sign for all present, known as the miracle of the sun. Jacinta and Francisco died within three years of the apparitions, but Lucia entered the Carmelite convent of St. Teresa and died when she was ninety-seven years old, having been given the responsibility of continuing to spread the messages of Our Lady.

. . . .

Basilica of the National Shrine of Our Lady of Fatima
LEWISTON, NEW YORK

"This is for you." My daughter is handed, by a complete stranger, a picture of the sky that undoubtedly is the background for an image of Mary. "It's from Medjugorje." I hear the man explain to another couple that he was taking pictures of their tour group in Medjugorje, and when he got the film developed, this image was in with the others.

We have stopped in the First Chapel of Our Lady of Fatima in Lewiston, New York, near Niagara Falls. Our Lady stands above the tabernacle, and the chapel is still used for personal consecration to Mary. The chapel is attached to the shrine gift shop, and in the shop, we find the familiar self-guided tour. It comes in quite handy, considering all that is squeezed into the area ahead.

The obvious first impression is of the number of statues all over the property. The walkways are filled with large stone, fiberglass, and bronze statues of saints and angels, Mary and Jesus. There are people working the grounds, planting flowers, and cleaning. As we walk up to one of the statues, the man working with the planting moves away, respectful of our time in prayer to St. Thérèse, my daughter's favorite.

The Barnabite Fathers came from Italy and decided to create a devotional center to honor Mary in the U.S. In 1954, with donations from generous benefactors, the farmland was given and the shrine started to grow to what it is today. We enter the basilica and can see what looks like a map of the world through the opaque ceiling of the dome. We easily find the Blessed Sacrament Chapel behind the right side of the altar. The crucifixion scene has at the base "Jesus I Trust in You." Inside that small space we find complete silence, complete peace, and his mercy.

Around the back of the basilica are stairs that lead to the top of the dome. As we climb, we can see clearly every aspect of the shrine. At the top is a thirteen-foot statue of Our Lady of Fatima with fresh flowers of thanksgiving around the base. As we look down, we see that the pond in front of the basilica forms a giant heart, Mary's Immaculate Heart, and the lights around the heart form a rosary with a huge marble corpus on a cross at the end near the pathway of the statues. Coming down from the dome, we begin taking our time walking the grounds and enjoying the area with the statues and the Stations. The appearances of Our Lady and the saints represent places from all over the world. She is for the whole world.

Mary wants us to know that it does not matter what we need or how we want to ask for help for our daily lives. Whether we go directly to Jesus with our prayer or feel more comfortable going through his mother or his saints or angels, prayer is what matters. Jesus gives us all of these wonderful people, especially his mother, to help us in this life. This beautiful place is a reminder of the gift of these great people who have gone before us, marked with the sign of faith, ready to stand with us in the challenges of this world. We stand overwhelmed by the goodness of our great God. Again, we can hear, "This is for you."

. . . .

Prayer

Mary, you entrusted the messages of Fatima to be delivered by three young children. In their innocence, they did not question the work that needed to be done. In their faith, they understood the importance of sacrifice. They simply obeyed their mother. Teach us to be obedient, to be trustworthy, to simply believe. Help us in our daily sacrifices for the salvation of souls. Help us to pray the rosary daily. And, in our times of doubt, remind us to get help from those who your Son has given, the saints and the angels and you, his mother.

. . . .

Grace

Jesus gave his mother, Mary, as well as the saints and angels, to help us persevere in this life. He gave his very life. Jesus loves us and so does his mother. They want us to be at our best. They give us every opportunity to be better, to love more, to make it to heaven. "This is for you."

. . . .

CHAPTER TWENTY-FIVE

Our Lady of Victory

The first shrine to Our Lady of Victory was built in France in 1213 after the French Crusaders won the Battle of Muret. However, Pope Pius V established the Feast of Our Lady of Victory after the defeat of the main fleet of the Ottoman Empire during the Battle of Lepanto in the sixteenth century. The Holy League credited the victory to the intercession of Mary. The rosary procession in St. Peter's Square that day was offered for the success of the Holy League. The defeat of the main fleet of the Ottoman Empire was critical to protecting the Catholic faith.

In 1629, the Augustinian Fathers built a convent in Paris, Notre Dame des Victoires. King Louis XIII funded the construction on the condition it be dedicated to the victory of the French at La Rochelle, attributed to the intercession of Mary. The church was enlarged in 1656, but confiscated during the French Revolution and used as a stock exchange. In 1809, Notre Dame des Victoires became a parish church with very few parishioners. The abbot felt he was a failure and was going to resign when he heard a request from the Blessed Virgin Mary to consecrate the parish to her Immaculate Heart.

He founded the Confraternity of Our Lady, Refuge of Sinners. The parish flourished, and thousands of pilgrims since have left offerings at the basilica in thanksgiving for answered prayers. Many famous people have prayed before the statue of Our Lady of Victory, including John Henry Newman, St. Therese of Lisieux, St. John Bosco, and Fr. Nelson Baker.

. . . .

Our Lady of Victory National Shrine and Basilica
LACKAWANNA, NEW YORK

The first thought we have as we drive up to Our Lady of Victory is, "Are you kidding me?" We have to wonder if we have driven up to one of the huge basilicas in Europe and not down Baker Street in Lackawanna, New York. The basilica is pure grandeur. The massive marble exterior is topped with copper domes (now green with patina from weathering), with the largest surrounded by four trumpeting angels who beckon us for Mass. We walk around to the front and admire the figures above the colonnades, which we discover later are Fr. Baker on one side and a Sister of St. Joseph on the other, with children. The original plan was to have a sculpture of a Brother of the Holy Infancy, but the artist and Fr. Baker's assistants changed the plan.

As we enter the church and wander down front with the rest of the community, we find it difficult to turn our attention from tourist to participant. The elaborate marble Stations of the Cross, the murals, the architecture, and the colors all lead to the center altar, backed by Our Lady of Victory. She stands above the tabernacle, crowned and adored by angels, presenting her Son to the world.

As I kneel, I simply take a deep breath. The morning has not been the best. I question dragging my family to so many places. They are tired, and it was not easy to get up this morning. And yet I hear plain and clear, "The victory is getting them here, getting them to the places, to the church to visit me. The rest is between them and me, between them and my Son." All I can do is to thank her and let the Mass bring us together as a family.

After Mass, we walk around the inside of the basilica. One of the parishioners explains that Fr. Baker had no money when he began this project in 1921 and yet finished it debt free in 1925. He wanted to build a basilica in honor of his patroness, Our Lady of Victory. He had visited Notre Dame des Victoires in Paris and prayed in front of her statue. With her help, Fr. Baker had added to St. John's Protectory and built an home for abandoned babies, as well as a hospital, nursing home, and trade school. He also saved an orphanage from financial ruin. His commitment was one of thanksgiving. This massive basilica is not only a symbol of one man's love and gratitude to Our Lady, but also a testament to the graces that Mary showers on those who ask.

Near the front altar, around to the side, we find a replica of the appearance of Our Lady to Bernadette in Lourdes. Below the stone, cave-like wall lays the tomb of Fr. Baker, and behind the main altar we find several other altars dedicated to St. Thérèse, St. Anthony, St. Anne, St. Aloysius, and Mary Immaculate. There is an altar dedicated to St.

Patrick, the name of the original church, and to St. Vincent de Paul—a model for Fr. Baker who dedicated his life to working with the poor. One of the parishioners takes us to the back to point out the beautiful baptistry, then steers us to the museum beneath the church. The priest and the parishioners share the same energy that we learn from the information gathered about Fr. Baker—energy used to spread charity and kindness and the gifts of grace from Our Lady.

Our Lady of Victory Basilica is breathtaking. The vision and dedication of this one man in one lifetime is nothing short of amazing. The graces given by Our Lady to those who ask work miracles. She leads us to her Son, and the life and the example of Fr. Nelson Baker leads us to believe that nothing is impossible with God.

· ·

Prayer

Mary, Lady of Victory, we come to you in constant battle with the world around us. Help us to persevere through our daily struggles. Help us to use our energies in charity and in love, to pray the rosary in your honor, and to trust that you will hear and answer our prayers. May we be examples of truth and of faith. Mary, intercede for us to your Son.

· ·

Grace

In our daily battles, in the constant struggles of life, big or small, Mary is here. She wants it all. She has the grace waiting for us to work through all of life's problems so that we can do the work of God, love one another, care for others, give to those in need. We just need to show up.

· ·

CHAPTER TWENTY-SIX

Nuestra Señora de la Conquistadora, Our Lady of Peace

. . . .

In 1680, the Pueblo Indians pushed the Spaniards out of Santa Fe, New Mexico. Twenty-one priests were martyred, and the Church of the Assumption was burned. The statue of Our Lady was saved and taken in the exile three hundred miles to El Paso. After about twelve years, Don Diego de Vargas was made governor. He visited the Pueblo Indians and spoke to them about peace, and they trusted him and agreed to let the Spaniards return to Santa Fe. The long march from El Paso took them until winter, and the Pueblos no longer wanted to leave. Outside the city, Don Diego built a shrine for the statue of Our Lady and prayed and went to confession. The people left behind prayed the rosary, while Don Diego and his men fought and finally regained Santa Fe.

The Cathedral of St. Francis was built in 1625 in place of the Church of the Assumption. The fiesta in honor of Our Lady continues today in June, when Our Lady is processed from the cathedral to the little rosario, the old campsite outside the city.

· ·

The Cathedral Basilica of St. Francis of Assisi
SANTA FE, NEW MEXICO

The Cathedral Basilica of St. Francis of Assisi stands in the center of the city of Santa Fe. Inside the beautiful basilica is the Chapel of La Conquistadora, Our Lady of Peace. Coming into life backward seems to be part of my story. We are not prepared to find this beautiful shrine of Our Lady. We have come to Santa Fe for a totally different reason, and as we walk around the peaceful basilica, we realize that she has led us where she wants us to journey. The statue of Our Lady, brought to the city from Spain by a Franciscan missionary, is decorated in dark red and blue, crowned and enshrined with a gold background and surrounded by images of saints. She stands as a symbol of love and of peace.

The Blessed Sacrament chapel is to the side of the main altar, set aside for quiet prayer amid a well-visited church. There is peace inside the door. We feel as if we are all alone, embraced by the heart of Christ. We pray to Our Lady to continue to lead us because we have no idea where we are going. We pray to her Son for protection, and we are grateful to them both for bringing us to this city filled with the gift of faith.

As we leave and go toward our car, we find behind the basilica the Stations Prayer Garden. The life-sized bronze sculptures are the work of a local artist. Again, we find peace. The city is packed, and yet we hear nothing. We are surrounded simply by the love of Christ.

. . . .

Prayer

Mary, we leave you in charge of our lives. We are safe in your mantle. We ask you to help us to put full trust in you for our journey. You give us the good things of life. You watch over us and care for us as Our Mother. Bring us to the peace that we can only find in your Son, Jesus.

. . . .

Grace

The cathedral looks really beautiful from the outside. Also, with our new Pope Francis, we have become more aware of the life of St. Francis and the call to build our lives in the Church and our faith in one another. The shrine of Our Lady of Peace is an unexpected gift. We are blessed in our visit. We are refreshed in our journey.

CHAPTER TWENTY-SEVEN

. . . .

Immaculate Heart of Mary

After the apparitions of Our Lady in Fatima to the three children, Lucia, the eldest, entered the Institute of the Sisters of St. Dorothy. Mary appeared to her again, putting one hand on Lucia's shoulder, while holding her heart, which was surrounded by thorns, with the other. The child Jesus stood beside Mary and told Lucia to have compassion for his Mother whose heart was surrounded by thorns pierced out of ungratefulness and sin. Mary blessed Lucia for trying to console her and asked her to promote her promise to the world to assist those at their death with the graces necessary for salvation.

All of these messages were sent in a letter to Pope Pius XII. Mary asked that we go to Communion on five consecutive first Saturdays of the month, go to confession, and say the rosary, making reparation for sin. She asked the Holy Father to consecrate Russia to her Immaculate Heart. In return for consecration, Our Lady promised to shorten the days of tribulations caused by persecutions of the Church. The pope instituted the Feast of the Immaculate Heart of Mary as one of the main feast days of the Church.

. . . .

Shrine of Our Lady of Peace Dedicated to the Immaculate Heart of Mary
SANTA CLARA, CALIFORNIA

Driving to California from Tennessee is quite an experience and an adventure that will linger in the minds of my two younger daughters for years. We have no reservations, no plan, just a destination and determination. We trust and, for the most part, all goes well.

We can see Our Lady well before we get to the Church of Our Lady of Peace. The thirty-two-foot stainless-steel statue stands among the buildings of the city and fares well for itself as far as catching the attention of those passing by. Monsignor John Sweeney commissioned the statue of the Immaculate Heart to be made in 1980 to bring honor to Our Lady. We are looking for a hotel for the night, visiting the shrine tomorrow, but pull into the parking lot of the church in time to witness the Sisters processing to the statue and gathering around Our Lady in prayer. We are all moved by the sight.

The next morning while visiting the shrine, we happen upon the end of a week of mission. The parish is run by the priests of the Institute of the Incarnate Word and their convent of sisters, the Servants of the Lord and the Virgin of Matara. The Mother Superior takes time to speak with us about the mission and Our Lady. The adults are gathered in the church listening to a talk, although a few are gathered for perpetual adoration, while the children are singing songs of the saints and learning to make rosaries. We are invited to make a rosary by one of the leaders, "You can pick your own colors."

Choices are something they have plenty of at this shrine. Every First Friday there is an all-night vigil ending at 5:00 A.M. on Saturday. On the thirteenth of each month from May through October there is a Mass in honor of Our Lady of Fatima. Every Tuesday there is Benediction, and there is the opportunity to visit the Blessed Sacrament every hour of every day.

As we walk to the statue of Our Lady of the Immaculate Heart of Mary, we are not alone. Quite frankly, we are never alone. And yet as we sit in front of Our Lady and she looms over us smiling, we feel that we are one-on-one with Our Mother. The church is appropriately named for peace because even with all that is happening, we are at peace. We can almost feel Mary's hand on our shoulders as we look at her heart surrounded by thorns.

She wants us, too, to receive Communion, go to confession, and pray the rosary. She wants us to know the pain in her heart when we sin. She wants us to receive the graces we need for salvation. She wants us, her children, to be with her forever, and she wants us to go out into the world and tell others so they too may obtain the promises.

. . . .

Prayer

Mary, your heart is surrounded by pain. Teach us your ways; help us not to sin. We are grateful for all you do for us, your children. Remind us in our hearts to talk to you, to thank you, to pray your rosary. May we spread your plea of frequent Communion and reconciliation. May we bring others to your heart.

. . . .

Grace

In this place so far from home, we are asked to participate in the journey. We are invited to a place at the table. There are choices in this place, and we are offered each and every one. In her heart, we are all family.

. . . .

CHAPTER TWENTY-EIGHT

Our Lady of La Salette

· ·

"Come near, my children, be not afraid."[12]

On September 19, 1846, on the Feast Day of Our Lady of Sorrows, Our Lady appeared in the small village of La Salette in France. Melanie Calvat and Maximin Giraud—children who had just met the day before in the fields—were watching over cows in the French Alps. They ate lunch and after a short nap went looking for the cows. After finding them, they returned to get their knapsacks and get back to work.

They both stopped, seeing a large globe of light. As they watched, the bright light cleared, and they could see a woman sitting on the stone with her elbows on her knees and her head in her hands. She was weeping. As she stood, the children could see she wore a pearl white dress with a full-length gold apron and a white shawl edged in roses. Her crown and slippers were trimmed in rose. Around her neck she wore a large crucifix with a miniature hammer on the right and pincers on the left. She told them to come over to her, and they hurried to her side. She was beautiful, and tears streamed down her cheeks as she spoke to them.

Mary's message was one of repentance. She did not want people working on Sunday and using God's name in vain. She told the children that she has prayed constantly for her people but that it is time for us to respond to her love with love. Mary then told each one of the children a secret that the other did not hear. She asked them to pray morning and night, even if only a Hail Mary and an Our Father, but whenever they could to pray more. She stressed that all were to go to Mass.

Mary walked to the top of the hill and said, "Now, my children, you will make this known to all my people." She gradually disappeared. Despite the hardships, the children delivered all of the messages from Our Lady. After five years, the apparitions were approved, and in 1879 the Basilica of Our Lady of La Salette, built where Mary appeared, was consecrated.

. . . .

National Shrine of Our Lady of La Salette
ATTLEBORO, MASSACHUSETTS

The messages at La Salette in 1846 are messages for today. We are so fortunate to be brought to this holy place. The world is full of great excuses for us to miss Sunday Mass and not have time for prayer. And we can always find reasons for why we struggle and why there is evil in the world. But what if this visit from Our Lady, this call to true continual reconciliation, this plea, could change everything? Our Lady takes the time to spend time praying for us and with us, and all she asks in return is for us to join her.

Our friend Jimmy has arranged for my husband and me to talk to the director and his secretary about the events at the shrine. After hearing about the Festival of Lights and the nativity display and the buses and more buses that come at Christmas and then again during the summer, we understand a little more about the hope for our world because of this place opened specifically to make Our Lady's messages "known to all [her] people." With this hope, we venture around the shrine.

The Rosary Pond is a place of prayer and meditation with a large standing crucifix that leads to the "beads" of the rosary. There is a peaceful calm, as we watch a group of special-needs young adults delight in finding fish in the pond. Mary asks us to pray a Hail Mary and an Our Father each morning and night and, if possible, more. We pray that everyone joins Our Lady in prayer. The world can be a better place.

The Garden of the Apparition is a place to listen. Mary weeps. Tears pour down her face. We need change. We need reconciliation. As she stands and reveals to the children the urgent messages, we too pay attention. We too are called to make them known. We climb the stairs and follow the crosses marked with Christ's love for us. She leads us to her Son. The third phase of her apparition sets us on top of the hill, and we can see all the different areas that make up the shrine. People should be told.

The Holy Stairs is a beautiful place for meditation. The tradition is that Jesus climbed twenty-eight stone stairs to Pontius Pilate. Many faithful pilgrims climb these stairs on their knees, contemplating the Passion of Christ. We witness the faithful.

The beautiful, large, white stations lead us around to a cave-like chapel commemorating where Jesus was laid in the tomb. Candles, flowers, and other items of special devotion line the walls. He has given his life for us. What can we do in return? It is time to follow the words of his Mother. We must reconcile, we must pray for conversion, we must make it known.

In the Shrine Church hangs a beautiful crucifix with a large hammer and pincers beside it. Mary wore the crucifix with the same symbols when she appeared. The message of the shrine is that the hammer is thought to represent sin, which nailed Jesus to the cross. The pincers, which remove the nails, symbolize reconciliation and prayer, which help to reconcile the world to God. "Be not afraid…make this known to all my people."

. . . .

Prayer

Mary, you love us. Help us to return that love. Help us to put aside all the excuses and go to Mass, pray, and reconcile with your Son. Our world today needs these urgent messages. Help us to step out of our own homes and go out into the world with your words of hope. Give us the courage and the strength we need.

. . . .

Grace

Together in the journey we hear the stories, and we believe. The message is right in front of us, and it is our challenge to spread the news. See how much she loves us!

. . . .

Conclusion

Our Lady dwells among us. She awaits a visit. Do not be afraid. She has gifts—treasures from her Son. She wants us to have the good things of life and the great things of heaven.

When we were young and visited our grandparents, my Grandmother Rose always had a little something for each one of us inside her cedar chest. Whether it was a Christmas gift she never used or something she purchased from the television or the store, she always had a gift for us—a small treasure that made us feel like we were her favorite. We never visited because of the gift, and we didn't always even like the gift. We took it because it made her happy and because we were grateful. We visited out of love, and we kept going back just to be in her presence.

Mary, too, is waiting for that visit from us. She has gifts right at her fingertips to offer as we go to her with our needs, with our time, and with our gratitude. Visit. Accept. Make your Mother happy. You will be glad you did.

Appendix

Marian Grottos, Shrines, and Basilicas
in the United States

ALABAMA

Cullman, Ave Maria Grotto

Hanceville, Our Lady of the Angels

Mobile, Cathedral Basilica of the Immaculate Conception

ALASKA

Anchorage, Holy Family Cathedral

ARIZONA

Hereford, Our Lady of the Sierras Shrine

Phoenix, St. Mary's Basilica

CALIFORNIA

Carmel, Shrine of Our Lady of Bethlehem

Colusa, Shrine of Our Lady of Sorrows

Laton, Shrine of Our Lady of Fatima

Santa Clara, Shrine of Our Lady of Peace

COLORADO

San Luis, Shrine of the Stations of the Cross

CONNECTICUT

Litchfield, Shrine of Our Lady of Lourdes

Waterbury, Basilica of the Immaculate Conception

FLORIDA

Miami, National Shrine of Our Lady of Charity

Miami, Our Lady of Guadalupe Shrine

Orlando, Basilica of the National Shrine of Mary, Queen of the
Universe

St. Augustine, Shrine of Our Lady of La Leche

GEORGIA

Atlanta, Shrine of the Immaculate Conception

ILLINOIS

Belleville, National Shrine of Our Lady of the Snows

Chicago, Basilica of Queen of All Saints

Chicago, Our Lady of Sorrows Basilica

Chicago, Shrine of Our Lady of Pompeii

Libertyville, Marytown, National Shrine of St. Maximilian Kolbe

Lombard, National Shrine of Mary Immaculate, Queen of the Universe

North Riverside, Mother of Mothers Shrine

Rockford, St. Mary Oratory

INDIANA

Leopold, Our Lady of Consolation

Merrillville, Shrine of Our Lady of Czestochowa

Rome City, Our Lady, the Immaculate Virgin Shrine

St. John, Shrine of Christ's Passion

St. Mary of the Woods, National Shrine of Our Lady of Providence

St. Meinrad, Our Lady of Monte Cassino Shrine

IOWA

Sioux City, Queen of Peace

West Bend, Grotto of Redemption

KENTUCKY

Carlisle, Our Lady of Guadalupe Shrine

Covington, Basilica of the Assumption

Hazard, Mother of Good Counsel Shrine

Louisville, Lourdes Rosary Shrine

Trappist, The Abbey of Our Lady of Gethsemani

LOUISIANA
Metairie, National Shrine of St. Ann
Natchitoches, Basilica of the Immaculate Conception
New Orleans, National Shrine of Our Lady of Prompt Succor
MARYLAND
Baltimore, Basilica of the National Shrine of the Assumption of the Blessed Virgin Mary
Childs, Our Lady of the Highway
Emmittsburg, National Shrine of St. Elizabeth Ann Seton
Emmittsburg, National Shrine Grotto of Our Lady of Lourdes
MASSACHUSETTS
Attleboro, National Shrine of Our Lady of La Salette
Boston, Basilica of Our Lady of Perpetual Help
East Boston, Madonna, Queen of the Universe National Shrine
Holliston, Our Lady of Fatima Shrine
Ipswich, National Shrine of Our Lady of La Salette
New Bedford, Marian Friary of Our Lady, Queen of the Seraphic Order
Worcester, Our Lady of Loreto Shrine
MICHIGAN
Detroit, Our Lady of Lourdes Shrine
Manistee, St. Mary's of Mount Carmel Shrine
Orchard Lake, Shrine Chapel of Our Lady of Orchard Lake
Pontiac, Immaculate Heart Shrine
Shrine Mio, Our Lady of the Woods
MINNESOTA
Coon Rapids, Epiphany Fatima Shrine
Minneapolis, Basilica of St. Mary
Sleepy Eye, Schoenstatt Shrine

MISSOURI

Carthage, Shrine of the Immaculate Conception

Eureka, Black Madonna Shrine and Grottos

Laurie, Mary, Mother of the Church Shrine

Nodaway County, Basilica of the Immaculate Conception

Perryville, National Shrine of Our Lady of the Miraculous Medal

Rhineland, Shrine of Our Lady of Sorrows

St. Louis, Shrine of Our Lady of Perpetual Help

Starkenburg, Shrine of Our Lady of Sorrows

MISSISSIPPI

Natchez, St. Mary Basilica

MONTANA

Butte, Our Lady of the Rockies

NEBRASKA

Boystown, Memorial Chapel of the Immaculate Conception

NEVADA

Wahpeton, Shrine of Our Lady of the Prairies

NEW JERSEY

Branchville, Sanctuary of Mary Our Lady of the Holy Spirit

Camden, Perpetual Rosary Shrine

Linwood, Shrine of Our Lady of Sorrows and of all Consolations

Little Falls, Our Lady of the Highway Shrine

Summit, Rosary Shrine, Monastery of Our Lady of the Rosary

Washington, Shrine of the Immaculate Heart of Mary, Apostolate of
   Fatima Blue Army Shrine

NEW HAMPSHIRE

Colebrook, Shrine of Our Lady of Grace

Enfield, Shrine of Our Lady of La Salette

NEW MEXICO
Chimayo, Lourdes of America
Mesilla Park, Shrine and Parish of Our Lady of Guadalupe
Santa Fe, The Loreto Chapel
Santa Fe, The Cathedral Basilica of St. Francis of Assisi
NEW YORK
Altamont, La Salette Shrine
Auriesville, National Shrine of the North American Martyrs
Brooklyn, Basilica of Our Lady of Perpetual Help
Brooklyn, Grotto Shrine of Our Lady of Lourdes
Brooklyn, Our Lady of Pompeii
Brooklyn, Regina Pacis Votive Shrine
Brooklyn, Shrine Church of Our Lady of Mount Carmel
Cheektowaga, Our Lady Help of Christians Shrine
Eastport, Shrine of Our Lady of the Island
Haines Falls, Shrine of the Immaculate Conception
Haverstraw, National Shrine of Mary Help of Christians
Lackawanna, Our Lady of Victory National Shrine and Basilica
Manorville, Our Lady of the Island Shrine
Middleton, National Shrine of Our Lady of Mount Carmel
Monroe, Rosary Garden Shrine
New York, The Lady Chapel, St. Patrick Cathedral
New York, Our Lady of Mount Carmel Church and Shrine
New York, Shrine of Our Lady of Pellevoisin
Pine City, Shrine of Our Lady Queen of Peace
Port Ewen, Boatman's Shrine of Our Lady of the Hudson
Staten Island, Schoenstatt Shrine
Stony Point, Marian Shrine, The Salesians of St. John Bosco
Youngstown (Lewiston), Basilica of the National Shrine of Our
    Lady of Fatima

NORTH CAROLINA

Belmont, Grotto and Pilgrimage Shrine of Our Lady of Lourdes

OHIO

Bedford, Shrine of Our Lady of Levocha

Bellevue, Sorrowful Mother Shrine

Burton, Shrine and Oratory of the Weeping Madonna of Mariapoch

Carey, Basilica and National Shrine of Our Lady of Consolation

Cleveland, Our Lady Queen of the Rosary

Cleveland, Shrine of Our Lady of Walsingham

Dayton, Our Lady of Lourdes Grotto

Euclid, Our Lady of Lourdes Shrine

Garfield Heights, Our Lady of Czestochowa Shrine

Ironton, Our Lady of Fatima

Lima, Our Lady of Fatima Shrine

Windsor, Our Lady of Guadalupe Shrine

Youngstown, Our Lady, Comforter of the Afflicted Shrine

OKLAHOMA

Bison, Our Lady of Fatima Shrine

OREGON

Lakeview, Queen of Peace Shrine

Portland, The Grotto, National Sanctuary of Our Sorrowful Mother

PENNSYVANIA

Allentown, National Shrine Center of Our Lady of Guadalupe

Donora, Shrine of the Holy Name of the Blessed Virgin Mary

Doylestown, National Shrine of Our Lady of Czestochowa

Fox Chase Manor, Our Lady of Lourdes Grotto

Harrisburg, Shrine of the Miraculous Medal

Kittanning, St. Mary, Our Lady of Guadalupe Church and Shrine

Loretto, Loretto Shrines, Our Lady of the Alleghenies Shrine

Olyphant, Shrine of the Miraculous Icon of Our Lady of Zhyrovytsi
Philadelphia, Central Shrine of the Miraculous Medal
Philadelphia, Our Lady of Victories Shrine
Philadelphia, Shrine of Our Lady of Knock
Saegertown, Roadside Shrine of Our Lady
Uniontown, Shrine of Our Lady of Perpetual Help
SOUTH DAKOTA
Alexandria, Fatima Family Shrine
Yankton, House of Mary Shrine
TENNESSEE
New Hope, Virgin of the Poor Shrine
TEXAS
Balmoria, Our Lady of Guadalupe Shrine
Dallas, Cathedral Shrine of the Virgin of Guadalupe
El Paso, Nuestra Señora de la Concepción de Socorro
Midland, Our Lady of Guadalupe Shrine
Port Arthur, Queen of Peace Shrine
Rockport, Mission of the Confidencia Shrine
San Antonio, Mission Nuestra Señora de la Purísima Concepción
San Antonio, Oblate Mission's Lourdes Grotto and Our Lady of
  Guadalupe Tepeyac de San Antonio
San Antonio, San Juan de Los Lagos
San Antonio, Shrine of Our Lady of Czestochowa
San Juan, Basilica of Our Lady of San Juan del Valle National Shrine
VERMONT
Isle La Motte, Shrine of St. Anne
VIRGINIA
Norfolk, Basilica of St. Mary of the Immaculate Conception

WASHINGTON
 Olympia, Our Lady of Perpetual Help Shrine
WASHINGTON, D.C.
 Washington, D.C., Basilica of the National Shrine of the Immaculate
  Conception
WISCONSIN
 Dickeyville, Dickeyville Grotto
 Hubertus, Basilica of the National Shrine of Mary, Help of Christians
  (Holy Hill)
 La Crosse, Shrine of Our Lady of Guadalupe
 Madison, Schoenstatt Shrine
 New Franken, Shrine of Our Lady of Good Help
 Twin Lakes, Shrine of Our Lady of La Salette
 Waukesha, Schoenstatt Shrine
 Wausau, St. Mary's Oratory of the Immaculate Conception
WYOMING
 Pine Bluffs, Statue of Our Lady

Illustrations

Notes

1. McNeil, Betty A., D.C., "The Journal of Mother Rose White: The Earliest History of the Sisters of Charity of Saint Joseph's, Emittsburg, Maryland," *Vincentian Heritage Journal*, Vol. 18: Issue 1, (1997), http://via.library.depaul.edu/vhj/vol18/iss1/2.

2. St. Louis de Montfort, *The Love of Eternal Wisdom*, 193, p. 37.

3. *Catechism of the Catholic Church* (Washington, D.C., USCCB, 1994), 966.

4. As recorded in Naples, 1773, by Fr. Marianus Ventimiglia, author of an ancient history of the Carmelite Order.

5. Quoted at www.ourlady33.myconsecration.org.

6. Quoted at Catholic Bulletin http://catholic-bulletin.blogspot.com/2009/03_01_archive.html.

7. Mike Amodei, "Our Lady of Good Help, Pray for Us!" *Engaging Faith*, https://www.avemariapress.com/engagingfaith/2011/01/our-lady-good-help-pray-us/.

8. Quoted in Michael Bie, *Myths and Mysteries of Wisconsin: True Stories of the Unsolved and Unexplained* (Guilford, Conn.: Globe Pequot, 2012), p. 5.

9. Quoted in Catherine M. Odell, *Those Who Saw Her: Apparitions of Mary* (Huntington, Ind.: Our Sunday Visitor, 1995), p. 48.

10. Quoted in Mark I. Miravalle, *Introduction to Mary: The Heart of Marian Doctrine and Devotion* (Goleta, Calif.: Queenship, 1997), p. 169.

11. Quoted in Raymond L. Burke, *Mariology: A Guide for Priests, Deacons, Seminarians, and Consecrated Persons* (Goleta, Calif.: Queenship, 2008), p. 848.

12. Quoted in William Bernard Ullathorne, *The Holy Mountain of La Salette: A Pilgrimage of the Year 1854* (n.p.: Ulan, 2012), p. 36.

ABOUT THE AUTHOR

Julie Dortch Cragon and her husband run St. Mary's Bookstore and Church Supply in Nashville, Tennessee. She is the author of *Bless My Child: A Mother's Prayer Book* and *Jesus at My Side: 365 Reflections on His Words.*